# Tender Hearts Rock Solid Faith

*I would like to dedicate this book to my husband, John. He has walked faithfully at my side through all of our joys and sorrows. I thank the Lord that you are my best friend and partner. I am incredibly blessed. Thank you.*

*Special thanks to my daughter, Stacie Richards, and dear friends: Michael Jackson, Sue Curd, and Rick Michels for all your support and help with this book.*

# Tender Hearts Rock Solid Faith

**How God gave a clueless young mother wisdom to raise godly children**

*A*dvantage
BOOKS

## Kitty Spencer

Avenue, Santa Ana, 92705–7016. Used by permission of Davidson Press, Inc. All rights reserved internationally

Scripture quotations marked TPT are from The Passion Translation®. Copyright © 2017, 2018 by Passion & Fire Ministries, Inc. Used by permission. All rights reserved.

Library of Congress Catalog Number: 2020939990


First Printing: August 2020
20 21 22 23 24 25    10 9 8 7 6 5 4 3 2 1
Printed in the United States of America

*Kitty Spencer*

# Table of Contents

# Foreword

# by Stacie Richards, author's daughter

Why This Book?

We were different.

We weren't really weird or anything, but we were kind of like a 50's family sitcom.

We had family dinners (and still do). We laughed together. We ate vegetables from the garden. We didn't have soda or sugary cereals in the house. We went to church and read our Bibles.

My brother and I went out during the summer days and came in when the sun went down. We played in the woods and made tree forts with our friends.

Why does all this matter? Because the stuff you will learn in this book really works and I am living proof.

One morning in April, 2018, I woke up to my husband of three years and asked him to help me. I was experiencing back pain like I'd never felt before. I was 36 weeks pregnant.

The pain escalated quickly. Soon I started to vomit from the pain, and dry heave when there was nothing left. "Call 911" I gasped weakly.

The ambulance came quickly and picked me up. At the hospital, they wheeled me directly to the maternity wing. My midwife arrived just a few minutes later, and said, "No time for pain relief --- you're fully dilated."

Within minutes, a tiny, slimy little person projected into the midwife's arms like a baseball into a catcher's mitt, and the midwife placed that tiny little person on my chest.

Like many women who go through the complicated physical, emotional and mental experience of birthing a premature baby, my emotions felt out of control.

This is where the contents of this book become important. There are a million self-help books out there, but this one can help prepare you (and your family) to face life's most difficult challenges with strength. The next day, an even more emotional event took place. I believe the faith I learned growing up enabled me to carry on with courage and strength.

The day after the birth, we were still in the hospital. My sweet little girl was being monitored because of her early birth and the possible effects from gestational diabetes.

It was joyful and emotional. I was nowhere close to getting this "new mom" thing down with the feedings every three hours and trying to master breastfeeding. I was tired already.

My husband received a call from my dad. "The medics are coming to take Mom to the emergency room."

WHAT?

"It's bad."

WHAT???

We found out later that night that a serious incident happened in her aorta and that the doctors said she'd die very soon. Surgery wasn't an option. Their estimate was that my mom had hours, or possibly just days to live. The plan of action was to observe her and keep her comfortable.

Within a week, still in the hospital, her blood count stabilized, and with no other options, they chose to send her home on hospice.

As my husband went to check on the situation, I couldn't help but cry. *I need my mom,* I pleaded with God. *I don't know how I'm going to do this without her.*

While feebly singing worship songs to the audience of my sleeping baby, my faith was strengthened.

*God, YOU ARE GOOD!*

*NOTHING happens beyond your control!*
*Soul, LEAN NOT on your own understanding.*
*God's ways are HIGHER.*
*God, NO MATTER the outcome, YOU ARE GOOD. I trust you. I put you above my feelings. You KNOW what you are doing. You are BIGGER than this situation.*

God gave peace beyond my understanding. Regardless of the outcome, God would never leave me or forsake me. He sees the beginning and the end of the story. His will and His ways are good!

I prayed for a miracle (oh BOY did I pray like never before), but my heart trusted that God would do what was best, no matter what.

THAT is why this book matters. It is chocked full of real-life stories and experiences that taught mom and us to really trust God. The legacy we leave are the children. Soon they will grow up and leave home, taking with them the values we instilled into them. Who will they be, and are they going to be able to cling onto God's goodness for their lives, their marriages, their trials and their own families?

That's exactly why this book is important.

I pray that as you read these words of wit and wisdom, your strength and your faith will increase.

*Kitty Spencer*

# Chapter 1

# We Really Want to Be Good Parents

"Who are you?" I pondered as I looked into the wide opened eyes of my newborn son. I was exhausted after ten hours of labor and a difficult delivery, but all that faded when I held this precious baby close to me. A little bubble of saliva formed on his lip and then popped. I watched in awe as the corners of his mouth turned upward in response. Could he be smiling? I chose to believe he was. Yep, he was amazing. Six minutes old and smiling; he must be a very gifted child.

With this baby in my arms, I wondered about who he would grow into. What would he look like? What would he do when he grew up? Would he follow Jesus all the days of his life? What kinds of joys and sorrows would he experience? I continued to muse as I thought about those controversies of nature verses nurture I had studied in some psychology class. Was he really a blank slate that would be written on by his environment? Or rather was he pre-programmed with his own nature which he was destined to live out? Was it some combination of both? It didn't take long to figure out he was not a blank slate. He showed us very quickly that he had his own ideas of what he did and did not want.

Our first challenge of the wills came within hours of his birth. My husband John and I were both sitting on the hospital bed with our baby between us. We wanted to change the diaper of this new little creature. It couldn't be that difficult. People had been doing this for ages. Besides, there were two of us and only one of him, and we had a lot of confidence in our ability to parent. We both came from loving families, we were college graduates, we had common sense, and we were committed to this child. However, our confidence quickly dwindled. We were not prepared for this confrontation. Our new son, Keith, did NOT, and I repeat, did NOT want his diaper changed. He was warm, cozy and comfortable, and wished to remain that way, thank you. As soon as we got his diaper un-taped, his mouth opened, and he let out a blood curdling scream. I reassured myself that we could not have stuck him with a pin because there were no pins. My mind quickly replayed everything we had done thus far. There was simply no way we could have hurt him. I looked down and saw his little tiny arms and legs flailing. Before we knew what happened, his heel dug into the dark, tarry, sticky contents of said diaper, and quicker than either of us could process what was happening, the tarry substance covered my husband's sleeve. Before I could even start laughing, which I had fully intended to do, his other heel was back in the dreaded tar pit, then more of it was on the sheet, then on my hospital gown. The more we tried to clean it up, the more we spread it around. The screaming and flailing of this newborn intensified.

A nurse happened to walk by our room at that moment and saw the scene at hand. I could tell she was trying to be professional and not laugh, but she was definitely amused. She quickly cleaned things up and gave us some good pointers on how to avoid this problem in the future. Yes, we got much better at changing diapers, but one thing did not change: for weeks, this child continued to let us know in no uncertain terms that he did not did not want his diaper changed.

As the days passed, I continued to ponder the responsibility of raising this baby. It seemed like a daunting task for us. We had never done this before. How do you take a completely helpless newborn, one who cannot do anything for himself, and turn him into someone ready to leave home and face this world in approximately eighteen years? Why does God choose completely inexperienced people to become new parents?

\*\*\*\*\*\*\*\*\*\*\*\*\*\*\*\*\*\*\*\*\*

Two years after Keith was born, we were blessed with our beautiful daughter, Stacie. Our two children filled our household with activity and joy. The years passed quickly, and before we knew it, my husband walked Stacie up the aisle and into the arms of a wonderful young man, Darin. We knew God had brought these two together, but my emotions were raw. This was even worse than leaving her in her dorm room the first time. After leaving her in her dorm room, we walked down that heart wrenching path back to the car, knowing that the doors of one precious season of our life were closing. This time, however, when we left her at the marriage altar, we knew we were really cutting the apron strings. This was our baby, and something just didn't seem right about letting her go. But it was right! It was just part of her growing up and time for me to buck up. And yes, my tears did eventually stop flowing, but it took a while.

I thought back over the years, and how in one sense it seemed as if it was only yesterday when we brought our first-born home from the hospital. In another sense, it seemed like such a long time ago. Had we prepared our children to launch out on their own and to be successful? What does it mean to be successful? I'd seen children leave home well equipped to get a good job and succeed financially, yet not be able to cope with disappointments in life. I watched on the news recently as young people rioted, started fires on a university campus, broke windows and injured people because they disagreed with a speaker who was scheduled to give a presentation that evening. These people had not learned how to respect others' points of view or to control their emotions. I'd been watching the violence and vulgarity during protests over a recent election. These people had not learned how to lose graciously. (Is this what happens when you give every child a participation trophy?) I've seen broken families where family members have gone years without speaking to others because of an offense. These people haven't learned how to forgive. Scripture tells us that the fear of the Lord is the beginning of wisdom. We wanted our children to be wise and of noble character. We wanted them to know how to respond to any situation with integrity. We wanted to raise them to honor God and obey Him.

In Deuteronomy 6:6, God clearly taught the Israelites that it was the job of parents to train their children to follow Him. He told them,

> *And these words that I command you today shall be on your heart. You shall teach them diligently to your children, and shall talk of them when you sit in your house, and when you walk by the way, and when you lie down, and when you rise. (Deuteronomy 6:6–7, ESV)*

It would be easy to slough off our responsibility and allow them to pick up values from television, movies, school, friends and such. We, however, believed God gave us the explicit command to train our children according to the tenants of biblical Christianity in accordance with scripture. We wanted to intentionally help them develop godly character qualities that would help them respond well to any situation they face.

The responsibility for raising children can be overwhelming, but we knew two truths that help set our minds at ease. The first was that we were not alone in raising them. One of the perks of being a believer in Jesus Christ is the fact that the Holy Spirit guides us. Can you imagine? The Holy Spirit, the Helper, the third person of the Godhead, the God of the entire universe lives inside of us and leads us.

*I will instruct you and teach you in the way you should go; I will guide you with My eye. (Psalm 32:8, NKJV)*

The second truth is that although God guides us and helps us raise our children as we partner with Him, He is the One who personally guides each of them. He is the one who ultimately forms their hearts and watches over them daily.

*From the place of His dwelling He looks on all the inhabitants of the earth; He fashions their hearts individually; He considers all their works. (Psalm 33:14–15, NKJV)*

Although we do the best we can to help them grow up well, we are flawed and won't do everything perfectly, but God is the perfect Father. He is doing everything right for them. Still, they have a free will and will make their own choices in life. Their choices are their own responsibility. Sometimes parents can do a great job raising kids, and the kids still rebel. After all, God was the perfect Father, and Adam and Eve still rebelled. Our job is simply to be faithful and trust God with our children. He loves them more than we do, and He will always do His best for each child.

My hope and desire for writing this book is to share some of our successes and failures as we raised our children. We want to pass along some of the insights and knowledge that came from our experiences, and to encourage others to trust in God. This book is divided into two parts: chapters two and three explain my personal journey of faith. God carried me through some very difficult circumstances and made Himself available and real to me. Because of this faith journey, I have a passion for God, and I want nothing less for my kids. I want them to experience the manifest presence, love and care of their Heavenly Father. The remainder of the book tells how God helped teach us to build godly character qualities into our children and to help them love God with all their heart, mind, soul and strength. Everyone's story is different. This book was written to tell our story of God's consistent faithfulness as we raised our children.

# Chapter 2

# First Love

When I was in elementary school, I had a friend named Chris Williams. I loved being with him and we spent much of our childhood together, but I thought he was nuts. No, I didn't just think he was nuts, I knew it. We would be out skating, walking, or bike riding, just having a good time, then out of nowhere, he would blurt out, "You need to be saved." He insisted that I must "receive Jesus." I thought that was a stupid thing to say. He would tell me this again and again. I had no idea what it meant, and frankly, I didn't care. He went on to tell me I that if I received Jesus, I could be sure I would go to heaven when I died. I knew that was ridiculous because I had always been taught you had to be good enough to go to heaven, and you wouldn't know if you had been good enough until you got there. I knew I was pretty good, at least better than Pat and Mike next door; they were always in trouble. And I did go to church every Sunday, so I knew that would help. I was pretty sure I was going to make it into heaven. *HA, and Chris said you could know for sure you could get there. That was just weird.*

By the time my children were born, my ideas about God and heaven had radically changed. Because of the events explained in the rest of this chapter and the next, I no longer thought Chris Williams was nuts. I began to understand what he meant by "receiving Jesus."

I did "receive Jesus" and I wanted more than anything else for my children to do the same. I wanted them to be content, have integrity, love others, have a good work ethic, have a Biblical worldview, walk in truth, love God with all their heart, mind, soul and strength and to love their neighbor as themselves. These traits grow as a result of abiding in (dwelling with and being connected to) Jesus, and the first step in abiding in Jesus was to "receive Jesus." The next step was to spend time with Him daily. I loved God, and I wanted my children to love Him as well, but I wasn't going to tell them every day that they needed to be saved. That was still weird.

> *I am the vine, you are the branches. He who abides in Me, and I in him, bears much fruit; for without Me you can do nothing. (John 15:5, NKJV)*

I didn't always have this passion for God. Yes, I had grown up going to church every Sunday and I cared about God, but at the end of my second year in junior college, my faith was challenged by a crisis in my family. I began to question God, His love, His goodness, and at times, even His existence.

This challenge to my faith began on a warm, spring day. I had just finished a long day of classes, and went to visit my mom in the hospital which was a few blocks from the college. She had been in and out of the hospital many times over the past several years because of intolerable headaches. This particular day, my dad was also visiting. As we were talking to her, she began coughing uncontrollably, and then she started screaming in pain, "I am going die, just like Josie!" Josie was her youngest sister. She had died mysteriously at age 28.

Mom was fading in and out of consciousness, and my dad ran to the hospital staff to get help. After what seemed like an eternity to me, the nurse and my dad returned to the room. The nurse took my mom's blood pressure. She said it had skyrocketed to three hundred and something over something else high. I can't remember. I didn't know exactly what the numbers meant, but I knew it was dangerous. The nurse left the room to get some assistance.

My dad was getting more and more agitated, so he went back to the nurses' station. I could hear my dad down the hall trying to "help" the situation along. He was frantic and was expressing his concerns at the top of his lungs. Everyone in the wing knew something was wrong. I just sat there, numb. I am sure everyone was doing everything they could to help, but to me, everything was moving in slow motion and no one seemed to be doing enough for my mom. I waited in the room with my mom for about ten minutes, at which time she went completely unconscious. I tried to get her to respond, but nothing. A doctor came in. They put her on a gurney and rolled her away. Dad went with them, but said for me to stay put. I felt helpless, scared, confused and alone. After waiting over an hour, I went to the nurses' station to see if I could get information. They told me they didn't know anything yet.

Instead of going back into my mom's room, I walked down the hall toward an exit sign. Outside, in back of the hospital buildings, there was a bench next to a large trash dumpster at the end of a long alley. It was almost dark, and no one was anywhere near this area. Normally I would be petrified to be alone in a place like that, but this time, I just didn't care. I walked to the bench, sat down, and cried and cried until there were no tears left. I prayed and prayed to the God I believed was out there somewhere until there were no prayers left. I worked my way back through what was now a very dark alley to the door which led back inside the hospital. I found a women's room and washed my face and took a deep breath and went back into my mom's room. Still no one was there.

Eventually, a nurse came in and told me what was going on. She said my mom had had a ruptured cerebral aneurism and was in surgery to stop the bleeding. I followed her to the surgery waiting room. My great-Aunt Margie was there. I ran into her arms and held on to her and wept. She was visiting from Florida, and I was sure glad she was there. She was one of my favorite people, and I just loved her. Needless to say, my dad was distraught and seemed to be in another world. His face was blank as he stared off into space. We waited. By the time the doctor came to update us, I looked at my watch and it was 7:00 a.m. the next morning. He said Mom had pulled through surgery, but he didn't know how much brain damage had occurred. All we could do was to wait and see. I know I was in shock and was not thinking straight, but I realized my first class started in forty-five minutes and I needed to be there. I wasn't hungry and I wasn't tired, so I figured the best thing for me to do was to walk over to the school and go to class. No one tried to stop me.

I absent-mindedly stumbled through my first couple classes as if I were on autopilot. Next, I went into the lab in the chemistry department where I worked. Two older ladies I worked with, Rini and Lita, took one look at me and asked what happened. I explained what had happened to my mom. They tried to comfort me, and then insisted I go home and get some rest. I reluctantly agreed and left.

The next several months were a blur. Mom was unaffected mentally by the accident. Physically, however, we had a long road ahead of us. She was weak and it was hard for her to control her leg muscles. With some assistance, she was able to walk, at least for the first month or so. We began daily trips to rehab, physical therapy, and occupational therapy. She was determined not to let this get her down. I specifically remember her saying she was not going to let this make her life small. I didn't quite understand what she meant by this, so she explained that she had seen other people with sicknesses allow these sicknesses to dominate every aspect of their lives to the point that they never talked or thought about anything else. She was going to stay interested in other people and their lives, and all the other things going on in life. I admired her for that.

The therapies continued and her condition worsened. She lost more and more control over her muscles. She got discouraged and extremely depressed, and I felt sick every time I came into a room with her. I hated what was happening. I just couldn't stand to see her suffer so much. Every night after dark, I went out and sat on the backyard swing and cried out to God for her to get better. I cried out for hope. There was none. After several months, she was completely paralyzed from the neck down. Scar tissue had been growing all down the spinal column and choked off the nerves. They discontinued all therapy. Dad tried to get some kind of nursing help for her, but for some reason unknown to me, he was unable to get any help at all. Dad, my twelve-year-old little sister Dolly, and I did what we could to take care of her. I went to a few classes at the junior college during the day, and then tried to do what I could to help around the house with cleaning and cooking afterwards, but I am sure I wasn't much help. I was depressed and grieving. Although my little sister was living there at the time, I was so self-absorbed I do not remember anything about how she was handling this crisis. I continued to go outside each evening and weep and cry out to God. Nothing improved. God was silent.

The semester ended, and I was home more during the summer. I became more withdrawn and miserable. I worked around the house, but avoided my mom as much as possible while still caring for her basic needs. Dad would put her on the couch in the mornings, and then go to work. I would feed her meals regularly and help her with a bedpan when she called. If she would fall off the couch, which happened frequently, I would have to wait until my dad got home to put her back on the couch. Many days she would lie on the floor for hours. She would cry and I would cry.

I wanted to do something to help her, so I began reading to her C. S. Lewis' space trilogy, *Out of the Silent Planet.* It seemed to lift her spirits. We both enjoyed that, but even before we finished the second book, her depression deepened and she no longer was interested in hearing any books read to her. She would just cry, and I could not stand to see her like that. Indeed, our lives had become small.

I needed to get away. I registered to begin school in the fall at Arizona State University, but after being there only a couple of months, I was completely falling apart. I couldn't concentrate on my classwork and hadn't made any friends. I had gotten a "C" on my last calculus test and it devastated me. I know that sounds silly now, but to me it was the straw that broke the camel's back. I had always done really well in school and I think I got my self-worth from getting straight "A's". Getting a "C" on a test was not acceptable. I was also feeling guilty for deserting my family. I didn't realize it at the time, but I was overwhelmed with depression. I quit school and went home.

Things hadn't gotten any better at home, but I continued plugging away at life day by day, month after month. I did what I could to help while feeling sorry for myself the entire time. I continued to pray, but felt God was not listening. I did believe God was real, but I did not believe He cared. Sometimes I thought He just enjoyed watching people suffer.

During this difficult season, I did continue to seek God. I attended the Newman Center, a Catholic campus church at Phoenix College. The Newman Center offered a retreat in Payson, which was about ninety miles from my home, so I went to it. I was doing everything I knew how to do in order to know more about God, but I left the retreat frustrated and without any answers. While riding the bus home, the words of a young lady next to me on the bus triggered a prayer that changed my life. She had looked out the window into the distance and said, "I just love Jesus." My mind started turning summersaults. How do you *love* Jesus? I had been going to church all my life. I wanted to love Jesus, but I didn't have a clue how to do that. How could I even know Him? I could not see Him, touch Him, hear Him, or smell Him. To me, He was some unseen, distant entity that was not reachable. Yes, He could probably see me and hear me, but I didn't much figure He'd want to bother. He had much more important things to be concerned with than my measly life. If He had heard my prayers, He certainly didn't care enough to answer them. Maybe He wasn't even real. Maybe God was just a big myth. Maybe everything I ever learned about God and Jesus was all wrong. How could she "love Jesus"? Even if He is real, maybe He is not good? He sure didn't seem good to me. My head continued to spin.

Her words impacted me in such a way that I prayed a prayer from the depth of my heart. "God, if You are real, reveal Yourself to me and teach me how to love You like this girl loves You." God answered that prayer! He did not answer right away, but upon looking back to that moment, I can see that after that prayer, my life took a 180-degree turn. Everything began to change. Decades later, I can look back and see that He absolutely taught me to know Him and to love Him.

I returned home after the retreat, but I still wasn't coping well. By the middle of the next summer I knew I needed to get away again, only this time I was determined to stay away. I was never coming home again, not even to visit!

I unexpectedly received a letter in the mail from Northern Arizona University. It was a full academic scholarship. I had not applied to the school, or for the scholarship. I am not sure why it was sent to me, but I decided to accept the scholarship, go to the university, and leave my family behind. I felt guilty about deserting them when they really needed me, but I wanted to leave. At this point, I just didn't care about anyone else. I stuffed the guilt way down in my heart and moved on.

School began and God began working in my heart. I found a job with a lovely Christian couple, Sue and Gerry, who loved me and nurtured me and began teaching me about the Bible. I believe God directed me to that particular job with those particular people. They are still very dear friends of mine. God began a process to shine the truth on a lie about the Bible I had believed for a very long time. You see, I knew you couldn't believe the Bible because I knew Genesis wasn't true. Scientists had proven it false, and if you couldn't believe the Biblical Creation story, how could you believe any of the Bible?

As a science major, I had fallen right in line with the naturalistic approach to creation. The story line goes like this: Billions of years ago and far, far away there was a big bang! Somewhere in the dark eerie outer edges of space a small planet emerged. The molten earth cooled as volcanoes and gases spewed out. Rain poured out from the clouds and washed down the slopes of mountains and formed the sea. This sea was a primordial soup of raw chemicals. Lightning hit the chemicals in this soup forming amino acids out of the raw chemicals. These amino acids joined together to create life itself. Over the next billions of years, these simple life forms evolved by natural selection into more and more complex forms of life, and eventually into human beings. I had no reason to doubt any of this because it was science and science was true and proven and fully illustrated in the textbooks. There was no longer a need for a Creator. It was possible for everything to have been created without God. At least that is what I believed.

One day, Sue and Gerry invited me to go to church with them, so I went. The Pastor was telling the Old Testament story of Joseph and his brothers. Joseph was his father's favorite son, and the brothers were jealous of him. God had given Joseph a dream about his brothers and parents bowing down to him. When Joseph told his brothers about this dream, their resentment of him intensified, and they sold him into slavery in Egypt. They told their father that wild animals had killed Joseph. God was with Joseph, and through a series of difficult trials for Joseph, God eventually promoted him to a position of second in command in Egypt. During a famine, the brothers had to come before Joseph in order to receive food. Joseph forgave his brothers, and God used this entire situation to save many people and to set apart for Himself the nation of Israel. I wanted to know more about Joseph's amazing God. At the time, I was unfamiliar with the Bible and asked Sue if this Joseph was Jesus' father. She politely said "no" and explained a little about the two Josephs. I continued attending church with them. I was enjoying the Bible stories their pastor taught and couldn't wait to hear more. On Sunday mornings I went to church with Sue and Gerry, and on Sunday evenings I went to my church, the campus Catholic Church.

While attending a Sunday evening service at the Catholic Church, the congregation was asked to hold hands while we recited the "Our Father." I joined hands with the young man next to me, John, not thinking much about it. After the service, he started up a conversation with me. We talked about different churches. I told him I was taking a Judeo-Christian Heritage class and needed to visit three different types of services to fulfill some of the requirements for the class. He invited me to go with him to a Seventh Day Adventist Church. I said, "Okay."

We attended the Seventh Day Adventist service together, and I really enjoyed it. The church also had a Friday night group, called Forum. John and I began attending the group in order to learn more about science and the Bible. Each week, a professor from the university would come and speak about some field of science, such as astronomy, geology, botany, zoology, etc. Each would show that what we see in the real world is consistent with what the Bible says about the world. I found this intriguing. We also went to a creation vs. evolution seminar at the university put on by a Creation Science organization. What I learned in that hour rocked my world. Could what I had learned about evolution be wrong? The evidence was compelling for creation and against evolution. I spent the next two years studying several books and videos about creation and evolution. [1] While investigating the claims of evolution, I found many inconsistencies in the theory.

---

[1] I studied the following books and video: *In the Beginning, Compelling Evidence for Creation and the Flood* by Walt Brown, Ph.D.; *Science and the Bible* by Henry M. Morris, Ph.D.; *The Mysteries of Creation* by Dennis R. Petersen, B.S, M.A.; *The Amazing Story of Creation from Science and the Bible* by Duane T. Gish, Ph.D.; a video called *From Evolution to Creation* by Dr. Gary Parker and *Creation Science Evangelism,* a video series by Dr. Kent Hovind.

The Evolution theory had so many assumptions that needed to be taken by faith. I eventually came to realize that it took as much or more faith to believe in evolution than it did to believe the Biblical account of creation. The conclusion I came to was that there was much more physical evidence to support creation than there was to support evolution. Just maybe the Genesis account of creation was true. Just maybe the Bible could be true, but I still needed more evidence.

I did believe God was real, and despite my investigation and appreciation of different churches, I still believed the Catholic Church was the true Church. I was unaware that my logic was a little skewed when it came to Catholicism. The Catholic faith was well ingrained in me and I believed in it with no hesitancy, but I still didn't know if the Bible was reliable or true. I was not about to put my heart and soul into believing some book unless I knew for sure it was true. So, I prayed, "God, if the Bible really is true, will You show me in such a way that I, with my doubting and stubborn heart, will know it is true?"

John, Sue, Gerry, and my new roommate Lynn, who also was a Christian, all believed the Bible, and tried to tell me that the Catholic Church taught things that did not line up with Scripture. I set out on a quest to show them the Catholic Church was the true church and everything I believed from Catholicism did indeed line up with the Bible. (I just didn't know which parts of the Bible were reliable.) I delved into Scripture and studied it daily. I began learning that a lot of things I learned in the Catholic Church were nowhere to be found in Scripture. I also learned that the Bible taught that the message of salvation and forgiveness and redemption were gifts provided and freely given because of Christ's substitutionary death on the cross.

> *For God so loved the world that He gave His only begotten Son, that whoever believes in Him should not perish but have everlasting life. (John 3:16, NKJV)*

*For all have sinned and fall short of the glory of God,* *(Romans 3:23, NKJV)*

*For the wages of sin is death, but the gift of God is eternal life in Christ Jesus our Lord. (Romans 6:23, HCSB)*

*If we confess our sins, He is faithful and just to forgive us our sins and to cleanse us from all unrighteousness. (1 John 1:9, NKJV, emphasis mine)*

*But as many as received Him, to them He gave the right to become children of God, to those who believe in His name: (John 1:12, NKJV)*

*My sheep hear My voice, I know them, and they follow Me. I give them eternal life, and they will never perish — ever! No one will snatch them out of My hand. (John 10:27–28, HCSB)*

These and many other verses kept swirling through my mind. Could the Gospel be that simple? Can I really admit I am a sinner in need of a savior, ask for forgiveness, turn from my sin toward Him and be born again into His family? Does He then forgive me and adopt me into His family, and give me a new Spirit and eternal life? Does He really have a plan for my life? Will He guide me, and communicate with me by His Holy Spirit and through His Word for the rest of my life? Will He truly never leave me or forsake me? Could it be that simple? I was still confused and not ready to take the plunge of pouring my life into believing that these things in the Bible were true. Nevertheless, the message the Bible proclaims was crystal clear to me. I just didn't know if I could believe it. And what do I do with all the teachings from Catholicism like having to be good enough to get to heaven? (How good is good enough?), no meat on Fridays, Novenas, penance, purgatory, the entire subject of saints and praying to them? The Bible called every believer a saint, not just the super good ones, and nowhere in Scripture are we encouraged to pray to them. In fact, the Bible said Jesus was the only mediator between God and man. My head was still spinning.

I had decided that if God would some how reach down through the universe and reveal Himself to me in a way that I knew for sure He was real and that the Bible was true, I would believe Him and dedicate my life completely to Him. I was simply not capable of making myself believe the Bible was true. If God didn't do something, I was just going to go on with my life without Him.

Meanwhile, my mom passed away. Although I felt a pit in my stomach and a wave of sorrow overwhelm me when I began to think about her, I pushed these feelings aside. I wouldn't let myself dwell on what had happened. I would quickly think about something else and went on with college life.

My dear friend John graduated from Northern Arizona University and moved to California, and I missed him a lot. I still had one year left in Flagstaff before I would be moving to Phoenix to do my internship. I would often scrape together what change I could in order to call John from the pay phone in the dorm hallway so we could chat. He would drive the 540 miles to Flagstaff to visit me whenever he could get enough money together and get time off work. We were good friends, but we knew our relationship could not go anywhere romantically because I would not marry a non-Catholic and he would not marry a Catholic.

I continued to seek God. I asked Him to somehow show me He was real and the Bible was true in a way that would convince me in the core of my being. Again, He was faithful and did just that. I began learning about the Old Testament prophets and how they prophesied about the coming Messiah. These Prophets wrote hundreds of years before Jesus's birth and yet they described things about Him and His heritage and His birth and His death in such detail, that only God could have orchestrated what was written.

My last year at NAU went by quickly. John, knowing I would be moving to Phoenix soon, moved there in November of 1980. I followed in January of 1981 in order to complete my degree by doing a one-year internship in the Radiology Department at Phoenix Baptist Hospital.

While in Phoenix, John and I looked into these prophecies and began studying them in detail. We also went to some Josh McDowell (Christian apologist, evangelist, world renowned speaker, and author) conferences and studied some of his materials. There were over three hundred prophecies concerning Jesus as the Messiah. There were a few that really penetrated my heart. For instance: Micah was a prophet who lived over 700 years before Christ was born, and he prophesied that the Messiah would be born in Bethlehem.

> ***Bethlehem Ephrathah, you are small among the clans of Judah; One will come from you to be ruler over Israel for Me. His origin is from antiquity, from eternity. (Micah 5:2, HCSB)***

That is a remarkable prediction. Other Prophecies described Jesus, the Messiah's lineage:

- ***Son of God (Psalm 2:7)***
- ***The Messiah would be from the seed of Abraham (Genesis 22:18)***
- ***Son of Isaac (Genesis 21:12)***
- ***Son of Jacob (Numbers 24:17)***
- ***Tribe of Judah (Genesis 49:10)***
- ***Family line of Jesse (Isaiah 11:10)***
- ***The House of David (Jeremiah 23:5)***

There were also many other prophecies about His death and resurrection including the following:

- ***Hands and feet were pierced (Psalm 22:16)***

- ***Crucified with thieves (Isaiah 53:12)***

- ***Cast lots for his tunic (Psalm 22:18)***

- ***His side was pierced (Zechariah 12:10)***

- ***Buried in a rich man's tomb (Isaiah 53:9)***

The list goes on and on. After studying the prophecies in the Bible, I became convinced that only God could have inspired the Scriptures. The completed Old Testament had been circulating around the known world for around four hundred years before Jesus was born, yet all these prophecies about Him in the Old Testament were completely and accurately fulfilled.

McDowell often told a story, in which his numbers were derived from reputable mathematicians, demonstrating the probability of these prophesies of the Messiah being fulfilled in one man. This could be illustrated by filling the entire state of Texas two feet deep with silver dollars, marking one of them with a marking pen, stirring them all together, blindfolding a man and having him walk anywhere in the state and choosing the marked silver dollar on the first try. The chances were 1 in 100,000,000,000,000,000. Those are pretty small odds. This is the same probability of one man fulfilling these prophesies concerning the Messiah being fulfilled in one man, yet all of these prophesies were fulfilled in Jesus.

I believed in the core of my being, that only God could have done that. I believed the Bible was true and accurate. God had answered my prayer, and I committed to making Him my Savior and my Lord. I committed to dedicating my life to Him.

Creation and prophecy may not convince everyone that God is real and the Bible is true, but I now believe with my whole heart that God revealed Himself to me in a personal way and He will also reveal Himself to anyone else who honestly seeks Him and is willing to submit to Him.

*And you will seek Me and find Me, when you search for Me with all your heart. (Jeremiah 29:13, NKJV)*

I still wasn't sure what to do with my belief in Catholicism and the teachings that were not taught in Scripture, such as purgatory, praying to saints, novenas, and penance. I was standing on a second-floor breezeway at John's apartment overlooking the swimming pool. I prayed and asked God to tell me what to do with my confusion over Catholicism. I clearly heard Him say in a still small voice, not audibly, but in my mind, "Let it go." I was overwhelmed with His presence and I felt a peace I had never experienced before. He went on to say, "Just continue in My Word, and believe Me." I said, "Yes, Lord," repented of my sin, and asked Christ to come into my life as my savior. I became a Christ follower. Little did I know this was just the beginning of a total transformation in my life.

I didn't know the trials I would soon face and how God would speak to me through His Word in the midst of the trials, bringing strength and peace. I didn't know I would learn to love Him just as the girl on the bus said she loved Him. He would truly become my "first love." I would learn all about that later, but for the time being, I had another important matter to contend with. I let John know of my conversion experience and it didn't take long after that for him to propose.

We were married a few months later, and we began attending a large, charismatic non-denominational church called *Valley Cathedral* in Phoenix. We continued to grow in our faith. We attended Sunday services, Wednesday night Bible classes, as well as a home group once a week. I also attended a women's Bible study which I believe set my marriage on a firm foundation and helped me avoid a lot of mistakes I otherwise would have made. In one of the studies, we talked about Psalm 27.

*One thing I have desired of the LORD, that will I seek: that I may dwell in the house of the LORD all the days of my life, to behold the beauty of the LORD, and to inquire in His temple. (Psalm 27:4, NKJV)*

That became my life verse and sent me on a road that I have always been grateful for. I made a commitment to spend time in the Word of God, to behold His beauty and listen to His voice every day from that day on. As I grew closer to God, He began revealing areas in my life that needed to be healed. I learned:

*For the word of God is living and powerful, and sharper than any two-edged sword, piercing even to the division of soul and spirit, and of joints and marrow, and is a discerner of the thoughts and intents of the heart. (Hebrews 4:12, NKJV)*

The Lord began a process of healing the layers of pain, sorrow, fear, bitterness, unforgiveness, and guilt that I didn't even know I was carrying. Some of the issues He delivered me from instantly and miraculously. Others He healed me through a process of changing my thought patterns over longer periods of time as I memorized Scripture and obeyed principles set forth in His Word. And yet other things He is still working on in my life.

# Chapter 3

# Transformed by the Word of God

One of the first healings I experienced occurred about a year after we were married. I was delivered from a lifetime of irrational fear. From the earliest days that I can remember, I was afraid of being attacked or kidnapped. At night, alone in my bed, even when my family was home, I often would shake in fear because I thought someone might break into my bedroom window. Every time I was home alone, I would lock all the windows and doors and tremble. I had a recurring nightmare of the backdoor of my childhood home not latching when I closed it, rendering the lock useless because you could just push the door open. Someone would be pushing it from the outside, and I would unsuccessfully try to hold it closed. This dream continued regularly on into my marriage.

I am not sure where this fear originated, but I suspect it had something to do with my mom's experience as a twelve-year-old. One time, I overheard her talking about being grabbed and almost being kidnapped by a man she had never seen before in a field on her way home from school. I didn't get any details of the story, but perhaps her fear stayed with her, and I subconsciously picked up on it. I also just recently learned about another incident from one of my aunts who had lived with us for many years. When she was in high school, back in the early 1950's, she witnessed a woman and her daughter being shot in their heads and killed just a few feet from where she was sitting on a city bus. In the midst of the chaos, she crawled out the window to get away. She told me that she mentioned it to her mom, who told her nonchalantly, "Oh, I guess you will always remember that." As far as I know, it was never spoken of again in the family until recently. She had apparently never gotten any help to deal with the trauma. Perhaps I picked up on some of her fear, too.

God completely healed my fear in an expected way. I had gone for prayer in the prayer room after a Sunday service at Valley Cathedral, our regular church. I asked for prayer for healing for back pain, but when the lady prayed for me, she commanded a spirit of fear to leave me. I thought that was really weird, but I immediately felt a heaviness leave me. I felt light and free. It was obvious to me that something had happened, but I didn't understand any of it. Jesus had often driven demons away in Scripture, and he commanded his disciples to do the same thing. That was too strange for me, and I really did not care to find out any more about it. I just knew something had changed. After that prayer, I never again experienced the fear of being alone, and the reoccurring nightmares never returned. The backache didn't go away, but the fear did. As I have learned over and over again, God does things His way, and I usually don't understand most of it.

Life went on, and we continued our Bible studies, home group, Wednesday classes and Sunday services. Life was good. We had two beautiful children and many wonderful friends. We were growing emotionally and spiritually, and everything was going well except for two issues. John was tired of the heat in Phoenix, and our finances left a lot to be desired. So, he went to a job fair and interviewed for a job at Boeing, near Seattle. I was not excited about this job prospect. I absolutely did not want to go to Washington, but I was beginning to learn to seek God's will over my own will. We prayed. I told God I did not want to go because all of my family was in the

Phoenix area, and I didn't want to be all alone across the country away from everybody. The next day, during my devotional time, I read,

**For whoever does the will of My Father in heaven is my brother and sister and mother. (Matthew 12:50, NKJV)**

God showed me I would have family wherever I went. John did get the job and God confirmed to us through several definitive ways that we should move to Washington. We packed up a rented moving truck, our one-year old daughter, our three-year-old son and our Shepherd-husky and headed north. God showed us quickly that we would indeed have brothers and sisters at our new home. We needed family and God provided.

John began his new job doing contract work for Boeing. Within a just a few weeks of being there, we found ourselves in a difficult situation. Stacie had been coughing quite a bit, so I decided to have her tested for TB. The doctors in Washington thought that was odd, but Stacie was eighteen months old, and it was routine to test for Tuberculosis at eighteen months in Phoenix, so they agreed to test her. Her test came back positive, and she had a spot on her lung. We immediately began treatment for her. A few days after this, I had a ligament rupture in my abdomen, resulting in severe internal bleeding. I had lost a lot of blood and was rushed into surgery. They said if I had arrived just minutes later, I would not have survived. They repaired the ligament and gave me six units of blood. I was incoherent for days. I remember seeing the clock in the room and feeling confused. I could see the numbers but couldn't figure out what time it was. I mentioned this to the doctor, and she said it would just take time to recover. A few days later, still very weak, I was able to go home. Shortly after arriving home, both children came down with chicken pox.

So here we were in a new city, knowing very few people. I was completely incapacitated and ordered bed-rest for at least six weeks.

Stacie had TB, both children had chicken pox. John had a new job and had to be at work or risk losing his job. I knew God would work things out, but I had no idea how He was going to do it. I prayed and waited to see how He would rescue us. And rescue us He did!

We had attended Silver Lake Chapel, a church near our new home, a couple of times. After I returned home from the hospital, several young moms from the church came by to see if we needed help. They assessed our situation and set up a team to help us out. They brought dinners and watched our kids in spite of our children having chicken pox. The TB was no longer contagious, so that was not an issue. They also came and cleaned house for us. We felt so blessed. For weeks, they took care of us in ways that far exceeded our imagination. I think about Stan and Jean bringing us fresh caught steelhead. I also think about Kay and Russ, Jack and Vicki, Kelly and Jerry, Mike and Sheli, and so many others who became so dear to our hearts. God met our desperate situation in a tangible way. Those who did the will of the Father were indeed our brothers and sisters in Christ, and we could not have asked for a better family.

The children recovered, and John's job was going even better than he expected. I recovered from the torn ligament, but continued to have other health issues. We lived in Everett for four years and stayed active in our church. Eventually we decided to buy a house rather than rent, so that led us to the small town of Granite Falls. Houses were less expensive there so we bought a house and moved again.

Adjusting to Granite Falls was challenging, but God continued to reveal Himself to us. I was having significant pain in my back, ribs, arms and legs. I tried to ignore the pain for as long I could, but finally went to the doctor. After several diagnostic tests and no answers, I was sent to specialist after specialist and still had no answers. My muscles were strained easily and I got hurt any time I tried lifting anything more than a couple pounds. It became more and more difficult to walk. Any time I did anything the least bit strenuous I would tear muscles and be left with large bruises. One of the doctors I was seeing gave me a pamphlet on domestic abuse every time I went in for an appointment. Another doctor said I might have fibromyalgia and chronic fatigue although he said the symptoms didn't really match the diagnosis. He thought, however, it would be worthwhile to experiment with a prescription that would help me sleep more deeply. The theory was that deep sleep would allow my muscles to repair themselves during the night. I decided to give it a try.

Within a few days, the pain had decreased significantly and I found I was able to do more without getting injured. It turned out that the medication was also an antidepressant. I hadn't realized that I had been extremely depressed, but the medication improved my mood considerably. I felt a lot better for a few months, and then started going downhill again. The depression was returning, only this time I recognized it as depression. I had a dark cloud that seemed to surround me. I constantly had this foreboding feeling that something horrible was about to happen and worry was my constant companion. No matter what was happening, I was certain the worst-case scenario would play out. If John was a little bit late coming home from work, I was sure he had been in a car accident. If one of the children didn't feel well, I was sure it was something really serious and probably incurable. If the phone rang after nine at night, I just knew it would be tragic news. And of course, that lump on my knee had to be cancer, and on and on it went. I began asking God to help me. He again answered my prayer and healed me emotionally and healed most of my physical issues. This time, however, the healing was not quick and some things got worse before they got better. It was a long process that would takes years and years of sitting at His feet and obeying each little revelation He showed me.

This change in me began in a Bible Study called "Walk Out of Worry." Kay, a dear mentor and still a dear friend, led this study and several subsequent studies for which I sat under her teachings. I learned that worry was a sin. It took a while for me to believe worry could be sin because worry was just normal for me. That is just what we did in my family. I didn't think anyone could help worrying, but God's Word said not to worry.

> *Cast all your cares upon Him, for He cares for you. (1 Peter 5:7, NKJV)*

It also said we were to:

> *Be anxious for nothing, but in everything by prayer and supplication, with thanksgiving, let your requests be made known to God; and the peace of God, which surpasses all understanding, will guard your hearts and minds through Christ Jesus. (Philippians 4:6–7, NKJV)*

Worry was a choice. I could trust God with situations, or I could choose to worry about them. I memorized these verses in 1 Peter and Philippians, and every time I started to worry, I would recognize the worry, pray about the situation and attempt to give the problem to God and leave it with Him. This worked to some degree, but I realized I had a much deeper problem. I did not believe God was good. God did not want me to continue to believe the lie that He was not good, and He continued to work in my heart. He had a lot of work to do. I had built up a pretty good case in my mind convincing myself God wasn't very good. I thought about how poorly God had treated His friends, after all, almost all of the disciples died horrible deaths as martyrs. Christians throughout the ages have been persecuted beyond belief. God did not help my Mom. How could He be good? How could I trust Him? About the time I was struggling with the idea that maybe God was not good, we got news that my cousin, who had just given birth to twins had died suddenly and unexpectedly at the age of thirty from a ruptured brachiocephalic artery. I remembered my two aunts, an uncle, my maternal grandfather and my mom had all died young and unexpectedly. With my cousin's death, however, came a diagnosis that shed some light on all these premature deaths. Our family had inherited a genetic disorder called Ehler's Danlos IV (EDS). There was no cure for it and no treatment for it. This was a serious and deadly disease that prohibited collagen from developing properly and left inherent weaknesses in blood vessels, arteries and ligaments. This disease was now affecting my generation. Shortly after my cousin died, we got news that her brother died also of a ruptured artery.

My older sister Carol got tested for the disease and came back with a positive diagnosis. She had been working as a neonatal nurse, but her health had also deteriorated over the years, and eventually she was unable to work. Before the diagnosis, the doctors just treated her as if she was a hypochondriac, and she was not able to get much help. After the diagnosis, they agreed to try to help her manage the pain, and she was able to get disability payments to help with her finances. She started on prescriptions of oxycodone and morphine. She struggled daily, and her life consisted of just trying to cope one day at a time. She would often fall and get huge bruises. She broke her hip, struggled to recover, and eventually got to where she could walk, albeit hunched over, using a walker. A major artery broke in her leg, taking months to heal. Almost all of her teeth had fallen out because the bones and ligaments would not hold them in. She was tough and extremely stubborn and continued fighting the disease with everything she had. She refused to give up hope of getting well during all of this. She lived alone and continued to do what she could to keep going. She refused to stop driving, even while taking the oxycodone and morphine. She had two pretty serious car accidents which left her body extremely crippled. (I have no idea how she managed to keep her driver's license.) Watching her suffer was heartbreaking, just as it had been heartbreaking to watch my mom suffer, but Carol was determined to make the best of it. Sadly, she succumbed to the disease and died of a ruptured aortic artery at the age of 62, almost two decades after being diagnosed.

Shortly after my sister was diagnosed with EDS, this disease affected my brother Danny. He had moved to Arlington, Washington, about twenty minutes from our home. It was nice having him close and he visited often. Our children loved having him around, and we did a lot of camping and boating with him. His favorite pastime was fishing, and we benefited from the many salmon and steelhead he caught. On January 29, 2001, I got a call from the school where he worked. He was the basketball coach, and he had failed to show up for their championship game. I knew something was wrong. He would not have missed that game for anything! I drove over to his house, praying for strength and listening to worship music the entire way over. I had hoped that one of his two cars would be gone, but when I drove up to his driveway, both cars were parked there. He had to be home. My heart sank. I could think of no non-disastrous reason for him to not have called work. I looked in the front window, hoping to see something encouraging, but not expecting to. The front door was open, so I walked into the house and looked around. I went into his bedroom. He was sitting on his bed with his back against the headboard and his feet on the floor and his hands in the air. My heart was beating so loudly I could hear it, and my mouth felt like cotton. I grabbed his arm. It was cold and stiff. There was no mistake. Now what? Think! Turn up the heater. It is freezing in here. I'll call John. No answer. I'll call the church. I can't find the number. I looked through my purse. Here is Aileen's number, my pastor's mom. I called her, and she said to hang up and call 911. I did. I told them what happened. Meanwhile, Aileen called Tanya, the pastor's wife who is a dear, sweet wonderful gal. Tanya brought another friend and came and stayed with me until the sheriff arrived. I am so grateful they came. What a blessing. I finally got in touch with John. He had ridden the bus to work, so he didn't have a car with him, but he was able to get a ride from a co-worker to my brother's house. I was so glad he finally arrived.

We answered question after question and filled out paperwork. My head ached. I was numb and in a state of disbelief. I called my dad to let him know what had happened. It was the hardest thing I had ever done in my life. I could barely talk. I could not bear to see my dad suffer another overwhelming loss. He had lost my mom and now Danny. Danny was his only boy, and Dad had dreams of growing old with my brother taking care of him. My brother was everything to my dad.

We waded through all that had to be done that night, and then picked up our children from church family who were watching them. I got home, went into the bathroom and just threw up over and over again. I prayed, "God, where are you? I can't stand this. I need Your help." Suddenly, an overwhelming peace and joy flooded over me. It was a supernatural experience. It was the same presence I felt when I was looking over the pool at John's apartment when I accepted Jesus as my Lord and Savior. The joy He gave me was not explainable in any human terms. His grace is sufficient.

This peace and joy stayed with me throughout the entire time we were planning the funeral and dealing with his possessions. An autopsy revealed that he too had died from a ruptured vessel which had been weakened by Ehler's Danlos. It was a very hard time, but the joy and peace I was experiencing continued to amaze me. I thought about how shortly before Danny died, he went to a men's conference with John. He went up to the front and gave His heart to Jesus and professed his faith in Christ's atoning work for his sin. God's timing was perfect. I thought about how I had just finished a book by Kathryn Hepburn in which she described finding her brother's body after he died. While reading it, I told myself I would never be able to recover from something like that, yet I did find my brother's body and was able to cope. My Bible study teacher, Kay Lindsey, had often said, "God doesn't give us grace for our imagination, but he does give us grace for our need." I found this to be completely true. God's grace was sufficient when I needed Him.

A few months after things settled from Danny's death, a new issue began to surface. I began having anxiety attacks. I was having difficulty sleeping, so I would go into the living room and try to sleep on the couch so I wouldn't wake up John. He had to get up every morning at four a.m. to go to work, and I didn't want to disturb his sleep. As I would lie on the couch, waves of anxiety would come over my body. My hands and feet would go numb. My heart would pound, and I would have a horrible sadness overtake me. This continued night after night.

I would get up each morning and put on a smile and plow through the day, doing what needed to be done. I prayed and asked the Lord if I should see a counselor and get help. I clearly heard Him say He would be my counselor and that I needed to continue in His Word each day and do what He showed me to do, and He would heal me. I told Him I would do that, but I didn't think He was doing a very good job of fixing things. He continued to show me He would be my counselor. He said:

> *For unto us a Child is born, Unto us a Son is given; And the government will be upon His shoulder. And His name will be called Wonderful, <u>Counselor,</u> Mighty God, Everlasting Father, Prince of Peace. (Isaiah 9:6, NKJV, emphasis mine)*

> *And I will ask the Father, and He will give you another <u>Counselor</u> to be with you forever. (John 14:16, HCSB, emphasis mine)*

> *But the <u>Counselor</u>, the Holy Spirit —the Father will send Him in My name—will teach you all things and remind you of everything I have told you. (John 14:26, HCSB, emphasis mine)*

I had nothing against going to a counselor, but for me, God had clearly told me not to see one. I also continued to pray that if at some point He did want me to get professional help, He would show me whom I should see. He did not show me anyone I should see.

During the wee hours of the night, I would turn on a small light and read His Word, His love letter to me. He began ministering to my soul and bringing me hope and life and light. He began showing me His goodness and love and began healing me in ways no human counselor could have. Psalm 130:5 and Psalm 130:7 popped off the page to me.

> *I wait for the LORD, my whole being waits, and in his Word I put my hope. (Psalm 130:5, NIV)*

> *Put your hope in the LORD, for with the LORD is unfailing love and with him is full redemption. (Psalm 130:7, NIV)*

My hope was to be in God and His Word. I knew at that moment I had hope. I wasn't stuck in this darkness and anxiety. God was beginning to do a deep healing of my emotions and my physical body. My entire thought processes and beliefs and habits were about to be radically transformed. I had previously often pictured myself getting so sick that I too would end up lying on the couch unable to get up, just as had happened to my mom. I now knew this was a lie from the devil to paralyze me and render me useless in the Kingdom of God. No, my hope was in God, and He is a powerful, loving Father. I read and memorized:

> *He is the Rock, his works are perfect, and all his ways are just. A faithful God who does no wrong, upright and just is He. (Deuteronomy 32:4, NIV)*

> *Surely your goodness and love will follow me all the days of my life, and I will dwell in the house of the LORD forever. (Psalm 23:6, NIV)*

I began memorizing verse after verse on God's goodness and His love for me.

I began understanding some of the tactics of the devil. When Jesus was in the wilderness, the devil would tempt Him, but Jesus always responded with "It is written..." and Jesus would quote Scripture, the truth. I began employing that response whenever I was tempted to see the future as hopeless and dark and dreary. I recognized that the battlefield was in my mind. When thoughts from the enemy would come, I learned to respond with the truth of the Word of God. For instance, if I would begin to think, "I am going to be so sick I will end up just lying on the couch every day like Mom." I would recognize that as the voice of the enemy and respond immediately by saying, "It is written,

> ***Surely Your goodness and love will follow me All the days of my life; And I will dwell in the house of the LORD forever. (Psalm 23:6, NIV)***

Fear and stress would be immediately lifted from me. If I would begin to think I could never be healed, then I would respond with,

> ***But He was wounded for our transgressions, He was bruised for our iniquities; The chastisement for our peace was upon Him, And by His stripes we are healed. (Isaiah 53:5, NKJV)***

> ***Bless the LORD, O my soul, and forget not all His benefits: Who forgives all your iniquities, Who heals all your diseases. (Psalm 103:2,3, NKJV)***

The truth is, God can heal me anytime He wants to. There is always hope. Maybe today He will completely heal me!

I would begin to think about some of the awful things happening in our government, then respond with,

> ***Rest in the LORD, and wait patiently for Him; Do not fret because of him who prospers in his way, Because of the man who brings wicked schemes to pass. Cease from***

*anger, and forsake wrath; Do not fret—it only causes harm. (Psalm 37:7–8, NKJV)*

Anxiety would instantly be lifted. My part was to obey God and stop fussing. If I would begin to think, "My life will never amount to anything," I would respond with the truth.

*The LORD will fulfill his purpose for me; your steadfast love, O LORD, endures forever. (Psalm 138:8, ESV)*

I would believe God and know that His purposes for me would be fulfilled.

During those sleepless nights and quiet times with the Lord with that small light and the Holy Bible, God spoke directly to me through His Word. God taught me how to overcome the hurt, guilt, anguish, depression, and pain that had built up in me over the years of seeing family members suffer and die. During this time, I memorized dozens of Bible verses God had shown me. Also during this time, God healed me emotionally, and my physical health improved dramatically. I still struggle physically with some pain, but not nearly as much as I had. I can do all the things God has called me to do. He also showed me practical things I could do involving food and exercise and supplements to help strengthen my body.

If I could start over with my children, in addition to the daily devotional time which we did each morning, I would make Scripture memorization a regular part of their daily life. I would get them each their own index card box, and when God showed us a verse that was pertinent to a situation they were experiencing, we would write it on a 3X5 card, memorize it, and make it part of a daily memory system. Each day they would get to work on memorizing the current verse and rotate through some of the old verses. It would only take a few minutes each day, and this system would keep all the verses they memorized current in their minds. Can you imagine the impact that could have on a young person's life, if this memorization process was a daily part of their routine, year after year? I personally have been doing this memory system with the verses I have learned for many years, and the benefits are innumerable. Unfortunately, I did not do this with my children, though I wish I had. I have precious grandbaby, and I plan to start this with her while she is very young. Hiding God's Word in our heart enables us to know God. I would recommend that every young mom incorporate a daily Scripture memory system into their children's lives. When God's Word is in their heart, our children cannot easily be swayed and driven off course by winds of false doctrine. When they leave home, you will know that they know God's ways.

After about a year after my brother had died, I gathered up the courage and got tested for Ehler's Danlos. I too was diagnosed with it, but rather than feeling crushed and fearful, God brought to my mind a verse I had memorized that brought me total peace.

*Indeed, we felt that we had received the sentence of death. But that was to make us rely not on ourselves but on God who raises the dead. (2 Corinthians 1:9, ESV)*

I realized that my life, like everyone else's life is completely in the hands of a loving Father. The peace I feel demonstrates again that His grace is indeed sufficient for any trial I have and will face, even a supposedly incurable, deadly genetic disorder. God is good.

The transformation that took place in my life as a result of "receiving Jesus" and spending time with God daily in His Word is such a testimony to God's love and His goodness. I want my children to experience God. My number one goal for them is for them to know God, develop godly character traits, and to be:

*Conformed to the image of His Son, (Romans 8:29, NKJV)*

# Chapter 4

# Contentment

"I need a "pooder, Mom," my three-year-old announced as he looked intently into my eyes. "A what?" I responded quizzically. All right, normally I am pretty good at deciphering "three-year-old talk," but this time I must admit I was baffled. His hands went on his hips and his foot stomped. This time, more emphatically he stated, "I NEED a 'pooder'!!!" He was getting desperate, and at this point I was helpless until his little one-inch pointer fingers started tapping into the air as if he were typing, and I got it. He thinks he needs a computer. I laughed and picked him up and told him how cute and funny he was, tickled his tummy with my nose, then set his little wriggling body down. He stomped off, probably figuring I was hopeless and would never understand how critical this was to his well-being. Nevertheless, I couldn't help but ponder what would compel someone who couldn't even say "computer" to think he needed one so badly.

A couple of weeks later I got my answer and understood why he was so sure he needed a "pooder." My brother, Danny, had moved into our house while he was looking for a job and a place to live. Along with my brother came television. Up to this point, we only had a few videos to watch with our VHS player and no reception on the TV. My brother signed us up for cable, and voilà –we had over

100 stations at our fingertips. Unfortunately, I soon learned I could set the children in front of a show and get so much more work done than I could with them underfoot. (Not really a good idea.) I put them in front of our new found babysitter. Then, right smack in the middle of a Tom and Jerry cartoon, there it was! Fisher Price had come out with a new toddler computer. Can you believe it? You could push the buttons on it and amazing things would happen. It could meow and moo and bark and you could make frogs hop. Of course, he thought he NEEDED this. All of a sudden it occurred to me that really, really smart people were spending millions and millions of dollars to make MY SON think he needed THEIR gadget. This was not fair!! How could I convince him he really didn't need a "pooder"? A seed of discontentment had been sown in his heart. He saw something he wanted and didn't have, and by golly, he figured he ought to have it! It's normal to stomp off when you are three years old and don't get what you want. It is the childish part of being a child. But part of training children is teaching them a better response to disappointment. We don't want them stomping off, throwing rocks, and starting fires when they don't get their way like some of the college kids I recently saw on the news. Contentment can be learned. The Apostle Paul learned to be content. Paul said:

> *I have learned how to be content with whatever I have. I know how to live on almost nothing or with everything. I have learned the secret of living in every situation, whether it is with a full stomach or empty, with plenty or little. (Philippians 4:11-12, NLT)*

Contentment did not come automatically for the Apostle Paul; it doesn't come automatically for us; and it doesn't come automatically for our children. It has to be learned. When we see something around us that we don't have, it is quite possible for an ugly little feeling to rise up inside of us and cause us to really want those things. We need to be aware of this response and guard our hearts against it. I am reminded of this principle from a story in Chuck Bentley's book, *Thrive – How to Do Well in Any Economy.*

> *Not too long ago an American company opened a new plant in Central America because the labor was relatively inexpensive. Everything went well until the villagers received their first paycheck; afterward they did not return to work. Several days later, the manager went down to the village chief to determine the cause of this problem. The chief responded, "Why should we work? We already have everything we need." The plant stood idle for two months until someone came up with the idea of sending a mail order catalog to every villager. There has not been an employment problem since!*

As this story demonstrates, it is easy to start wanting things we see and don't have. That is not always a bad thing, but when we notice discontentment and frustration brewing inside of us or inside our children, it is time to step back and evaluate what is going on. Materialism is everywhere in our culture. Every commercial on television or the radio is designed to tell us our life would be so much better if I just had the right hair color, or drank the right beer, or owned a "pooder," or bought whatever else they are selling at the moment. We are all vulnerable. We need to be aware of the snares that are around us and around our children. It takes effort to teach our children to be aware of these snares, and then to be content with not getting everything they want. When my son sees this amazing toddler computer, of course he is going to want it. It is natural for him to want it, but God's ways are supernatural. As parents, we need God's wisdom to be gently molding God's character into these precious little hearts. But how do we do that? It is not an easy task, but I believe we found three strategies to help our children learn, like the Apostle Paul did, to be content in every situation.

Unfortunately, it was years into the process before we learned these strategies. I wish we would have learned them sooner. I admit it, he got the "pooder" and most of the other things he thought he needed. It would have probably helped him more to learn that he would have survived without many of them. Lesson learned: They need to learn early not to throw fits when they can't have something they want. The following three strategies will help children learn to be content:

## Strategy #1 Thankfulness

Training a child to be content is not an easy task, but I believe I found one of the secrets to doing so many years ago while walking through Na 'Aina Kai Botanical Gardens, one of the many stunning Hawaiian parklands. The flowers were the largest and most beautiful I'd ever seen in my life. The fruit and nut trees were remarkable, and I felt like I was in paradise. It made me wonder how the Garden of Eden in the Biblical story of creation must have looked. I could only imagine how Adam and Eve must have felt. They had everything they could have ever needed, and they had each other. Above all, they walked in the cool of the evening with God Himself in a perfect garden. In spite of the many blessings, what did Eve focus on? She focused on the one thing she could not have—the forbidden fruit. I used to wonder why she ate that fruit when she has so much of everything else. I don't wonder any more. I am pretty certain I would have done the same thing.

As I look back over my life, I see many times when I was blessed abundantly, and instead of being thankful, I foolishly focused on something I wanted, but didn't have. I had good friends and family, good teachers, and good health as a child. I had plenty of food and a good home, but I wasn't thankful. Instead I focused on what I didn't have. I was not content.

In elementary school, I thought I was too skinny. I was obsessed with my weight and regardless of what I ate, I remained skinny. Just like Eve, rather than being thankful for what I had, I thought about one thing I couldn't have and this made me miserable. In junior high school, I thought my nose was too big and let my stupid obsession with it ruin those years. By the time I got to high school, I had grown up a bit and was getting more comfortable with how I looked, but I still wanted something I couldn't have. I wanted to be able to sing well. I had zero musical ability and couldn't carry a tune, and no matter how hard I tried, I still could not sing so I moped around. I felt cheated because I didn't get what I wanted. I again wasted a lot of time being unhappy instead of focusing on and being thankful for what I could do well. I think I would have been right there with Eve, discontent and wanting the one thing she couldn't have, rather than focusing on all the good things around her.

In a book called *The Hiding Place,* by Corrie Ten Boom, this principle is well illustrated. In this true story set in Holland during World War II, Corrie and her family were arrested for hiding Jews in their home during the Holocaust. She and her sister Betsie were sent to Ravensbruck, a concentration camp in the center of Germany. The circumstances were agonizing. It was crowded, cold, damp and miserable. The food was insufficient, the work was merciless, their health was failing, and to top is off, they were being eaten alive by fleas. Corrie complained to her sister, Betsie. Betsie gently reminded her of the Scriptures Corrie had shared with the women in their barracks earlier that day: Rejoice always, pray without ceasing, give thanks in all circumstances; for this is the will of God in Christ Jesus for you, (1 Thessalonians 5:16-18, ESV). Betsie and Corrie decided immediately to look around for things to be thankful for. They were thankful they were together. How much worse would the situation be if they didn't have each other to lean on? They were thankful they had been able to smuggle a Bible into the concentration camp. The Bible was God's Word and it brought them hope and light in the dreadful situation they were in. They were thankful for the overcrowding because that gave them an opportunity to share the gospel of Jesus Christ with so many people. They continued month after month looking for things to be thankful for. This thankfulness improved their attitudes and rubbed off on other women as well. The entire atmosphere in their barracks changed for the better.

As a young mom, I did not want my children to make the same foolish mistakes that I had made. I wanted them to look for all the good things around them. I did not want them to focus on what they couldn't have or couldn't do. As parents, you can set an example and thank God verbally for your own blessings in front of your children regularly. Then, every night while tucking them into bed or during some other part of the day, ask them to think about their day and tell you something they are thankful for, regardless of whether they had a good day or not. By doing this you will help them establish the Biblical pattern of being thankful which increases contentment.

> *Finally, brethren, whatever things are true, whatever things are noble, whatever things are just, whatever things are pure, whatever things are lovely, whatever things are of good report, if there is any virtue and if there is anything praiseworthy—meditate on these things. (Philippians 4:8, NKJV)*

## Strategy #2 Generosity

I don't know why God chose to bless me so greatly, but I am grateful He does, and I don't take it lightly. I want my children to realize, too, how blessed they are. People all over the world lack food and clean water. There is so much pain and suffering in our world. According to UNICEF, between 26,500 and 30,000 children die each day because of their poverty. [2]

---

[2] https://library.cityvision.edu/global-poverty-statistics (accessed September 19, 2019)

When our children are exposed to some of the realities that exist outside of their little circle of concern, they get a different perspective and begin to see how blessed they are. Things that they used to complain about often don't seem to matter as much anymore. Taking their eyes off of themselves and looking at the plight of others around them can inspire thankfulness and compassion and generosity in them. When they understand the difficulties of others, their hearts change. I do not want them to be crushed by the poverty and suffering in the world around us, but I do want them exposed to it. I want them to appreciate what they have and be thankful. I also want them to know they can help others who have not been so richly blessed. One of my pastors often said, "Whatever you wish you could do for everyone, do for someone."

There are endless opportunities to teach kids to serve others. Participating in one of the ministries that reaches out to children in need can help our children to connect globally to a child living in poverty. We can sponsor one or more of these kids through organizations like *Food for the Hungry* or *World Vision.* Our children can send pictures, write letters, and even send some of their own resources to reach out to another child. When they understand how blessed they are and become thankful, it compels them to give to others. As they become generous, they become content and begin to understand the love of God.

As a family, we can donate or volunteer at food banks, serve Thanksgiving, Christmas, and Easter dinners at local men's and women's shelters or local churches. If possible, go on mission trips. We can fill up a shoe box with school supplies and gifts and send them out with *Samaritan's Purse.* My family especially enjoys giving chickens as Christmas gifts through *World Vision,* allowing impoverished families to provide food for their families and to make a profit from egg production and sales. At the church where my son worked, during Christmas time, each employee was given a check to use to bless someone in the surrounding community. This creates an atmosphere of love and giving that continued to grow, even beyond the Christmas season.

You may be saying to yourself, "Can this work in my house with my children? Can it drive out discontentment? Can it help with a teenager in crisis?" After all, it is a well-known fact that when hormones wake up, sometime around age thirteen, the hormones go right to the brain and turn off every brain cell connected to rational thought and reason. Emotions move in and take over. Goodbye, my sweet little adorable compliant daughter. All right.... I made that up. It is not really a fact, but I would bet that a national poll of parents of teenagers would report that hormones cause something strange to happen to brain cells. What made sense to kids when they were ten seems to be beyond their ability to comprehend just a few years later. I suggest that being generous with one's time, energy and resources can radically change anyone, even a teenager who is sure the world is going to end because she doesn't have the right pair of jeans and shoes and it is your fault.

The following story my daughter wrote in high school illustrates how thinking about and helping others impacted her during her turbulent teenage years:

## What I Did on My Spring Break

By Stacie Spencer

*If you were to ask a high school student what she would like to do the most during Spring Break, how do you think she would respond? What if she said she would like to spend the week cleaning up the city and devoting her time to various service projects around the community? Would you be surprised? Can you imagine a hundred high school students not only saying they would like to do this, but actually doing it? I was part of a Spring Break project called "Conspiracy of Hope" that did just this each Spring Break from 2000 to 2006. My involvement in "Conspiracy of Hope" had a huge impact on my life and taught me how much difference a group of people with a common goal can make in a community and in individual lives.*

*In the year 2000, Jim Romack, a local pastor in Granite Falls, Washington, decided to create a backyard mission trip for students to serve in this small community and communicate the love of Jesus in a tangible way to a community that needed to experience that love. So during the Spring Breaks of my junior high and high school years, over a hundred high school students came from many cities across Washington State to Granite Falls and painted downtown business buildings, picked up trash, cleaned the houses and yards of the elderly and offered a Bible day-camp which was attended by over two hundred elementary age students. Out of the many community service events that I have participated in, this has been the most meaningful to me because it was a concentrated effort to change people's lives.*

*One example of a changed life is an elderly woman named Lolly. We cleaned her house, did yard work and visited her. Her husband had recently died of cancer, she was not well, and her dog had died that morning. Her loneliness, grief and depression were devastating. Our visit with her that day was life changing. She continued many of those friendships and became part of a church where she is now loved and cared for.*

*One person can make a difference. Hundreds made a lasting change. "Conspiracy of Hope" showed that teens aren't just consumed with video games, junk food and laziness, but that they want and like to help out the world around them. They can effect genuine change.*

*"Conspiracy of Hope" impacted the community both tangibly and eternally. Not only did the students beautify Granite Falls, they gave much needed help to many elderly people, and they brought a new hope into the community. They showed that high school students can be hardworking, considerate and joyful. They demonstrated to the community that serving others with no donations accepted and no strings attached is a noble way to live. "Conspiracy of Hope" taught me that people working together can accomplish much. These Spring Break mission trips birthed in me a vision of how I'd like to continue serving others my entire life. I could have slept in during my Spring Break, but this this was much more fun and rewarding.*

Encouraging our kids to be generous with their time and resources does create changes in their hearts. It does help them to be content. Just start. Start with a decision to give to others and make it a part of your family tradition. As we practice generosity, it will become a way of life for our children.

## Strategy #3 Fearfully and Wonderfully Made

Contentment comes not only from being thankful and generous, it comes from knowing that God created a masterpiece when He made the person our child sees in the mirror. He made each of us unique with gifts He has given us in order to fulfill the calling He has placed on our lives.

*For we are God's masterpiece. He has created us anew in Christ Jesus, so we can do the good things he planned for us long ago. (Ephesians 2:10, NLT)*

Young people often feel inadequate. They may look around and see others that are smarter, better looking, better at sports or at any number of other things. They see people on TV or in magazines that are gorgeous, with perfect bodies, and they foolishly compare themselves to these not so real images. Comparison is always a bad idea. If we think we are worse than someone else in some way, we feel short changed. If we think we are better, we fall into pride. It is a lose/lose situation. The truth is, we are all created incredibly exceptional.

The Book of Job has a good lesson in it that demonstrates just how unique each one of God's creations is. Even the ostrich, which definitely has its issues, is an amazing creation.

*The ostrich flaps her wings futilely, all those beautiful feathers, but useless! She lays her eggs on the hard ground, leaves them there in the dirt, exposed to the weather, not caring that they might get stepped on and cracked or trampled by some wild animal.*

*She's negligent with her young, as if they weren't even hers. She cares nothing about anything. She wasn't created very smart, that's for sure, wasn't given her share of good sense.*

*But when she runs, oh, how she runs, laughing, leaving horse and rider in the dust (Job 39:13-18, The Message)*

When I first read this about the ostrich, I had to smile. "But when she runs, oh, how she runs." The specific touch of the Creator on the clumsy ostrich is remarkable. Oh, how she runs, faster than the horse and rider in fact. I can just imagine God looking at His finished ostrich creation and saying to Himself, "Well done! What a marvelous creature I have designed, O how she runs." This is amazing, and yet how much more astounding is each of God's kids? Each child is designed in the image of God and has infinite value because of it. Like the ostrich we may have some kind of shortcoming or disability, but there is also something in every one of us that causes God to say, "What a marvelous person I have designed. Look how she… or look how he…" (you fill in the blank.) Part of the privilege of being a parent is to help our kids discover their unique, God-given gifts and calling. We can declare with the Psalmist:

*For You formed my inward parts; You covered me in my mother's womb. I will praise You, for I am fearfully and wonderfully made; Marvelous are Your works, And that my soul knows very well. (Psalm 139:13-14, NKJV)*

A precious young friend of ours, Tessa, was able to handle a challenge that came her way because she knew that she was created special and God had a purpose and a plan for her. She was sixteen years old when her hair began falling out in chunks. Alopecia would be hard for anyone, but when a girl is sixteen it can be catastrophic. Coming from a God honoring family who consistently walked in faith, she turned to God during this time of trial. She took her eyes off of herself and thought about other children who had alopecia. She decided to do a school project to inform others about the condition and to raise money for the Alopecia Foundation. She presented an assembly for the entire Granite Falls High School to educate them about the disorder. She then arranged for several barbers to come to the gym after school and set up hair cutting stations. Next, she invited any student, their parents, and any other community member to come and for a small donation to the Alopecia Foundation have their heads shaved in solidarity for Alopecia sufferers. Tessa and her dad were the first to have their hair shaved off. Over a hundred people followed. People were lined up for hours. Tears were shed, and our community of Granite Falls, Washington came together again, in support of a young lady and her dream to help others.

God says each of us is fearfully and wonderfully made. Remind your children again and again how precious they are in God's sight. Remind them that God is good. Remind them that He has a purpose for them, and that He loves more than we can even comprehend. He sees the big picture of their life, and He doesn't make any mistakes. When this truth gets inside our children, they can gracefully withstand life's difficulties.

*Kitty Spencer*

# Chapter 5

# Truth

*I have no greater joy than to hear that my children are walking in the truth. (3 John 4, NIV)*

I had always thought of myself as a truthful person - until one day while sitting in the dentist's chair. It was as if my eyes were suddenly open, and I realized I had told an out and out lie! I hadn't even realized I had lied until several minutes later. Why did I answer "yes" when the dentist asked if I flossed every day? I flossed often, but not every day. The more I thought about it, the more I realized there could be at least two reasons I just lied. The first one is that I am a people pleaser, and I had formed a habit of just saying what I thought people wanted to hear. The dentist wants people to floss daily so that is what I said. The other reason could be that I wanted people to think well of me. I formed a habit of exaggerating in order to make myself look better. After realizing these things, I asked God to make me aware of every time I lied out of convenience or habit. He did; He began helping me break this perpetual habit. I would say something like, "It took me two hours to finish the dishes," when it in fact only took half an hour. I could hear the Holy Spirit prompt me, "Really, two hours?" Why did I say two hours? It was just a habit to exaggerate. Two hours of working sounds better than half an hour.

Once I was aware of this problem, I often caught myself telling stupid lies. God was faithful in pointing them out to me and helping me to change. I have come a long way, but change in me is still a work in progress.

Lying is far too common in our culture, and it is easy to justify. I picked up a reprint of a small book titled, *Ethics, An Early American Handbook*[3]. It was originally published for young public school children in 1840. These children were deliberately taught what truth is and to tell the whole truth in all situations. While reading the chapter on truth, I realized it is very easy to purposely deceive someone else without admitting to ourselves that we are lying. One evening, during our weekly home group consisting of adults who were mostly in our fifties, sixties, and seventies, I read aloud the chapter on truth to them.

Lies were categorized under the following five headings, but they have one thing in common. They are all meant to deceive.

1. Saying a thing when we know it is not true.

2. Saying a thing when we do not know whether or not it is true.

3. Prevaricating.

4. Misrepresenting.

5. Exaggerating.

All of these are different forms of untruth. Each one of us in our home group recognized that we had fallen into some of the pitfalls of lying.

Although this was a children's book, I have to admit that not one of us in our group knew what prevaricating was, but we were going

---

[3] Comegys, Benjamin B., ed, *Ethics, An Early American Handbook*, (Boston: Ginn & Co., 1891)

to find out. Each of these categories was explained through stories in a way that was easy for young children to understand.

**1.** The first story illustrated a category of lying entitled "Saying a thing that is not true." This story showed how slightly avoiding the truth is dishonest, and it usually has a way of eventually turning into a web of untruths. These untruths have a way of getting one into such a trap that he will either need to admit he was dishonest, or he will need to tell a direct lie in order to continue covering up his dishonesty.

The boy in this story used his dad's axe to cut a hole in the ice in a pond to go ice fishing. The axe slipped from his hand and fell into the hole and under the ice. The father was not able to find the axe and asked his son to look for it. The proper response would have been to admit to the father immediately that he had lost the axe. The boy, however, went and looked for the axe. He didn't actually lie, but neither was he being honest.

Later in the day, the father asked if the boy had seen the axe lately. He had to answer quickly and the son said "No." He again justified his dishonesty. He told himself he wasn't actually lying. He hadn't seen it for hours. His dad said, "Lately." Surely "lately" must have been more recently than early morning. He was getting more entangled in this falsehood.

Eventually, his dad asked if he had seen the axe anytime since they had been splitting logs together. He said, "No, sir." He couldn't tell the truth now without exposing all his previous dishonesty. He had now told an outright lie.

Most children understand that telling an outright lie is wrong. However, their understanding can get a little fuzzy when it comes to subtly misleading others. They need to understand that any deception, even a small one, is wrong. Also, small deceptions usually lead to more dishonesty to cover up the first dishonest behavior. It is important to help our children understand that any deception is wrong, not just actual, verbal lies. They can avoid a lot of distress and heartache and embarrassment by simply being forthright and honest in all situations. Deliberately teach them to look at their intentions and their hearts in each situation, not just their words. This will save them a lot of trouble in the long run.

**2.** "Saying a thing when we do not know whether or not it is true" is another common form of deception. Someone who would not say something he knows is false may say something that he thinks or hopes might be true. The ethics book gives the example of a father asking his son if the cows are in the barnyard. The boy had seen them there earlier in the day and did not want to bother going out to check to find out if they were still there, so he simply said, "yes." He thought they were there and hoped they were there, but he really didn't know they were there. This falsehood was not a direct lie, as it would have been if the he knew the cows were not in the barnyard, but it still was not the whole truth. Our kids need to be taught this difference. Left to their own, they can easily think something is not a lie if they just think it is true. Teach them to focus on being completely truthful.

**3.** "Prevaricating" is not a common word; it is, however, a common form of deception. How many times have you looked into a child's eyes and seen the little gears cranking in his head as he tries to think of just the right words to explain something without actually lying? Prevaricating means saying words that are true, but convey a false meaning. The book tells of a boy who says he does not have a single nut in his pocket, when he actually has many nuts in his pocket. It is true, he does not have a single nut in his pocket, but he is not being truthful. Another example is the child who answers "No" when asked if he walked to the store while his parents were gone. Technically, he is correct in saying no because he actually rode his bike to the store. He may be saying words that are true, but he is not being truthful because he knows his parents really are asking if he went to the store. Another example is a child who says he did not eat all the cookies, when he knows he ate all of them except the one he gave to his dog. Again, that is theoretically true, but not honest. We as parents must teach him that this is just as wrong as deliberate lie. We want our children to learn to walk in integrity at all times. We want them to be trustworthy. We want to deliberately teach them what prevaricating is and teach them not to do it. They can understand it is so much easier and better for them if they just start out with the truth.

Many politicians have mastered the art of prevarication. Imagine a government run by people who always tell the whole truth, rather than just what is technically true, but essentially dishonest. Imagine our government being populated with statesmen, people who were more interested in doing the right thing than saying just the right words to please people (and to protect themselves legally). Imagine people who do not prevaricate when they run for office, but tell the entire truth. We would not have anywhere near the amount of corruption we see in our nation. We should teach our children to be that kind of person regardless of the career they choose. They can be world changers.

**4.** I recently observed a superb example of the fourth category of untruths mentioned in the Ethics book: Misrepresentation. I was sitting in the waiting room of a doctor's office when a young mom walked in with a baby and two boys roughly two and five years in age. The mom went to the front desk carrying the baby, and the two boys proceeded to the play area. The two-year-old sat at the table playing with some blocks. The five-year-old observed for a while, then walked over and took all the blocks from the younger child. The younger child looked at his brother in the eye, and with a sad expression on his face, got up and went to play with a small wooden truck from the toy box. Soon afterwards, the older child took the truck from the little one. The little one lowered his head and walked away again. This time he picked up a small book from the shelf, only to have that snatched from his hands. Finally, enough was enough! The little guy leaned over and quickly bit his brother's arm hard enough to elicit a loud scream from Mr. Big Shot. I'm thinking, "Way to go, Little Man." Mr. Big Shot runs to mom. She asked what happened. He says, "Eric bit me. I was standing next to him and he leaned over and he bit me." Yes, it is true that Mr. Big Shot was standing next to his little brother, and his little brother did lean over and bite him, but he left out some of the details. This is what a misrepresentation of a situation looks like. I admit, I couldn't keep my mouth shut. I asked the mom if she wanted to hear the rest of the story. She fortunately said "yes," and Mr. Big Shot learned very quickly that misrepresenting the situation was not good for him.

Unfortunately, misrepresenting situations has become commonplace. When I watch news stories from differing networks with differing points of view, I am often appalled at the number of details omitted because of the network's biases. I am appalled at the amount of dishonesty I see. Imagine a news station run by people who completely and honestly report the news faithfully. Imagine them not leaving out the details that support a point of view that opposes their perspective. Imagine honest, unbiased reporting. We need to teach our children not to misrepresent any situation they talk about, whether they become journalists, or not. Truth matters.

**5.** Sometimes it seems exaggerating, our fifth category of lying, is a great American pastime. Exaggeration makes stories more fun and more interesting. Exaggerating can make people sound more heroic than they actually are. By exaggerating about not feeling well, a child who may just have a slight headache can convince his mom he is really sick and needs to stay home from school. By saying he tried as hard as he could, when he actually put very little effort toward doing a math problem, a child can get out of doing it. There are endless advantages to exaggerating, but it is still a form of lying.

It is important to help our children know exaggeration is a form of lying and that it is wrong. Help them be people with integrity.

> *Teach me Your way, O LORD, that I may walk in Your truth. (Psalm 86:11, ESV)*

God's Word teaches us that truth is important. Truth is something we must deliberately teach our children. They must understand that saying things are true when we don't know for sure they are true; saying words that are true but convey a false meaning; misrepresenting a situation; and exaggerating are all forms of lying and need to be avoided. When our kids consistently walk in truth, they will stand out. They will impact others. They will be warriors who make a difference in their generation.

## The Truth Shall Set You Free

It is not only important to train our children to speak the truth, but also to know the truth. In today's world of Google, social media, news, twitter, biased textbooks, etc., we get bombarded with an unbelievable amount of information. Some of it is true, and some of it is not. I would love it if all information came with an infallible banner that said "TRUE" if something really was true, but it doesn't. Even the fact-check sources can't be trusted.

There are ways to set up some safeguards for protection from being swept away by false ideas. Jesus said something very interesting while He was speaking to Pilate. He said,

> *Actually, I was born and came into the world to testify to the truth. All who love the truth recognize that what I say is true. (John 18:37, NLT)*

Scripture is called the Word of God. Scripture also tells us that Jesus is God. He came to us in the flesh in the form of a baby.

*And the Word became flesh and dwelt among us, and we have seen his glory, glory as of the only Son from the Father, full of grace and truth. (John 1:14, ESV)*

We have access to the Word made flesh: the Scriptures. The Scriptures are Truth. Filtering what we see and hear through the words of Scripture can help us eliminate a lot of confusion.

*If you continue in My word, you really are My disciples. You will know the truth, and the truth will set you free. (John 8:31–32, HCSB)*

One example of confusion which is prevalent in our culture today is sexuality. Gender identity, homosexuality, and marriage are areas wrought with misunderstanding. The granddaughter of a friend recently came home from kindergarten with a look of concern on her face. She had a note in her hand saying she would need remediation in reading. While her dad was reading the note, the little girl went on to explain that she learned that she could marry a girl when she grows up and that she herself might not actually be a girl. Really! Apparently, there was not enough time for her to learn to read, but there was enough time for her to be indoctrinated in something that wasn't even true. Our culture and our laws may say she can marry a girl, but it is not the truth. God designed and defined marriage.

*Therefore, a man shall leave his father and mother and be joined to his wife, and they shall become one flesh. (Genesis 2:24, NKJV)*

Two women taking wedding vows with each other is not marriage, regardless of what the courts say. The grandparents above knew they needed to do something to protect this precious little one from this lie and began praying about finding a solution to the problem.

If God is real and the Scriptures are true, then we as believers have a transcendent standard to measure our beliefs against. As believers, we can hold up a standard of absolute truth. Our God created the universe and knows how it works. He knows what is best for us. He knows where we will find peace, and He knows how a society functions the best. Although we live in a fallen world and there are a lot of opinions regarding gender identity, homosexuality, marriage, and many other subjects, Scripture is not ambivalent. If we believe God, we don't have to be confused. If our children believe God, they can be rescued from the misinformation that surrounds them.

God created the world and created mankind. He knew exactly what He was doing and He wasn't confused. He told us about gender identity in the book of Genesis.

> *So God created man in His own image; in the image of God He created him; male and female He created them. (Genesis 1:27, NKJV)*

God created two genders. At the time I am writing this, there are roughly thirty-two genders being recognized by society. This is absurd, yet many people believe it, especially the ones who have been through college where this kind of thinking is commonly communicated to impressionable young people. In the books of Matthew and Mark in the New Testament Jesus repeated this truth.

> *And He answered and said to them, "Have you not read that He who made them at the beginning 'made them male and female." (Matthew 19:4, NKJV)*

> *But from the beginning of the creation, God made them male and female. (Mark 10:6, NKJV)*

Some people may believe they were born in the wrong body. One may think he is really a woman in a man's body or a man in a woman's body. That is a very difficult position to be in. It can be painful and frustrating, but the truth is, none of us are in the wrong body. The DNA in every cell of our bodies testifies to the truth about which gender we are. Pretending to be a different gender or even changing the outward appearance of one's gender does not change the facts.

Also, some people are attracted to people of the same sex, but God says this is not right and it is not the best for us. He only wants what is best for us. True peace will only come by aligning ourselves with God's truth. We have a choice. We can believe God or we can be like Eve in the garden and believe the enemy when he says, "Did God really say…?"

*Now the serpent was more crafty than any of the wild animals the LORD God had made. He said to the woman, "Did God really say, 'You must not eat from any tree in the garden'"? (Genesis 3:1, NIV)*

This is one of Satan's oldest tactics and many of us still fall for it. He tempts us to question God's Word. God says He created us male and female. To deny our gender or to choose to marry a person of the same sex is to NOT believe the God of the Bible. God gives us the choice of believing Him or not believing Him. He does not force us to believe, but, just like Eve, we do have to live with the consequences of our choices, and our society reflects those choices.

I completely understand same sex attraction. As a child, and throughout my teenage and young adult years, I longed for a mother's affection. My mom was very ill most of my childhood, and I never felt she was able to give me the nurturing I desired. As a child, I would imagine that the women in some of the television shows were my mom. I would live out adventures with them in my mind. They would show me the affection I longed for. My imagination would run wild. In high school, I was involved in theatre where homosexuality was very common. I could have easily chosen that lifestyle. However, because most of culture condemned it, and I really wanted to do the right thing, I did not embrace that lifestyle. Just deciding to not pursue a homosexual lifestyle, however, did not bring me peace. I still struggled with a longing I thought could be filled by a woman's love. This went on for many years and the feelings would not go away. I lived with inner turmoil. On the outside, I did not pursue women, but I still allowed my imagination to go unchecked. I could not understand what was wrong with me or why I was so miserable.

It wasn't until I believed that the Bible was true and that God had the power to set me free, that I found freedom. While reading God's Word, I learned that homosexuality was sin and that I needed to repent and turn completely away from every form of it.

*Do you not know that the unrighteous will not inherit the kingdom of God? Do not be deceived. Neither fornicators, nor idolaters, nor adulterers, nor homosexuals, nor sodomites. (1 Corinthians 6:9, NKJV)*

*Likewise, Sodom and Gomorrah and the cities near them, which like them committed sexual sins and engaged in homosexual activities, serve as an example of the punishment of eternal fir. (Jude 7, ISV)*

I knew I could no longer allow my imagination any room to think about being fulfilled by the love of a woman. That was an empty promise from the enemy that would only bring more heartache. Would I believe God or would I believe my feelings? I chose to believe God in spite of my feelings. Only God could fill that emptiness, and I knew I wanted to obey Him. I repented and completely turned from these longings, imagination and all. I chose to believe His way was best, regardless of what my feelings were telling me.

*For He satisfies the longing soul, and fills the hungry soul with goodness. (Psalm 107:9, NKJV)*

It took some time, but eventually my God delivered me completely and set me free. He satisfied my longing soul. As a result,

I have a wonderful and completely fulfilling relationship with my husband, and I have a wonderful family.

God's Word can bring clarity to any issue we face and any questions we have. God says He will give us wisdom when we ask Him and He says He will personally guide us. Can you imagine, the God who knows absolutely everything will give us wisdom? God is so good. The following two verses are great memory verses to teach our children. God says He will guide them whenever they ask Him. By memorizing these Scriptures and hiding them in their hearts, our children will embrace a precious gift they can carry with them for the rest of their lives.

> *If any of you lacks wisdom, let him ask of God, who gives to all liberally and without reproach, and it will be given to him. But let him ask in faith, with no doubting, for he who doubts is like a wave of the sea driven and tossed by the wind. For let not that man suppose that he will receive anything from the Lord; he is a double-minded man, unstable in all his ways. (James 1:5–8, NKJV)*

> *I will instruct you and teach you in the way you should go; I will guide you with My eye. (Psalm 32:8, NKJV)*

If our children continue in God's Word, they can indeed walk in the truth and the Truth will set them free!

As our children grew in the understanding of God's Word, they also began reading more about the world and different cultures. Reading became a huge part of our family time. They began seeing God's truth verified in the world around them and began developing a world view based on a solid foundation.

# Chapter 6

# Reading

When my brother Danny moved into our house and connected our TV to cable, we learned something about ourselves and about our children. We learned that we did not have as much self-control as we thought. We learned that we had difficulty resisting the television. Reading to the children, a nightly habit of many years, changed overnight. We suddenly found ourselves mysteriously drawn to that talking picture box. I have a theory that I am sure no one else in the world would agree with and there is zero evidence for, but I think it has to be true. There must be a very large brain magnet in that TV, and corresponding small brain magnets in each one of our brains. It sucks us to the couch right in front of the television. It was so easy to just turn on the set and vegetate in front of it each evening. We formed a new habit of watching television. Our old habit, reading, which had impacted us in so many good ways, went out the window immediately and didn't come back until we disconnected from the cable about six months later. Without the cable, we got back on track and re-captured our precious family time.

We had begun reading to our children every night when they were babies and continued it well into their high school years (except for the six months we had cable TV). It is something that we did right! It is something I cherish and would recommend to any family if at all possible. The dividends were far greater reaching then we ever imagined when we began.

Every night, we settled into our comfortable bedtime routine, a routine we and the children immensely enjoyed. They put on their pajamas and brushed their teeth, then snuggled up with us for stories. In the beginning, we read from all kinds of picture books. We later read a series of Christian character-building books for young children. One series, by Michael P. Waite, included *Handy-Dandy Helpful Hal*, a book about helpfulness; *Max and the Big Fat Lie*, a book about telling the truth; *Sir Maggie the Mighty*, about obedience, and several others. The *Adam Raccoon* books by Glen Keane, parables about following Jesus, were another favorite. *Frog and Toad*, Amelia Bedelia, Judy Blume's character Fudge, and Laura Ingalls from *The Little House on the Prairie* all felt like they became part of the family. For all of us, this was our favorite part of the day.

We were not aware of some of the benefits of reading to the children when we began this nightly habit. One important reading skill is the ability to picture stories while reading, as if one is watching a movie. Studies have shown this ability is enhanced when children are read to.

I did not read very much and had not been read to as a child, and I had not personally developed this skill. As a result, it was not unusual for me to read an entire paragraph and not remember anything I had just finished reading. While taking some classes on how to teach children to read, I learned how to overcome this insufficiency. It was a long process, beginning with learning to visualize one word, then one sentence, and so on until one could picture an entire story. I practiced these new skills and got better at it. As a result, my comprehension improved dramatically.

As we read to our kids, they seemed to automatically visualize what was being read. I remember one time I did not think Keith (who was about eight years old at the time) was listening to a word my husband was reading, so I asked him what was just read. Keith repeated the entire last scene with startling accuracy. I asked him how he could remember all those details. He said, "I could just see it in my mind." I was impressed. I questioned my daughter on various occasions, and found she was able to do the same thing. This skill is priceless.

Another skill they inadvertently seem to develop was a remarkable attention span. In this era of short sound bites, scenes on the screens flashing in quick sequence, and fast video games, it takes effort and practice to train our brains to slow down, stay focused and work hard. By the time they were in second grade, they could listen attentively for extended periods of time. Sitting for more than an hour and listening was very easy for them. This is not overly common among this age group, but we knew it was something good for them, and we were glad they loved to listen to the stories. We also noticed that their vocabulary was expanding.

As the kids got older, the books got longer and their world view grew. We read true stories about people from all over the world from various time periods. They lived the adventures of Harriet Tubman as she helped slaves escape through the Underground Railroad. They learned of Mary Slessor, a small red headed Scottish missionary who went to Africa in 1876. Because she earned the trust of the natives, she was able to spread Christianity and protect native children from death and other unbelievable atrocities. We read about George Muller, who in the late 1800's rescued over 10,000 orphans from the streets of London and cared for them. He set up five orphanages, and never asked for money. He and his wife prayed and God provided every single need for every single child. What a lesson on faith and prayer! Because of all the children George Muller rescued, The Daily Telegraph, a British Newspaper, wrote that he "... had robbed the cruel streets of thousands of victims, the gaols (jails) of thousands of felons, the workhouses of thousands of helpless waifs." We read about John Wesley, Gladys Aylward, John Newton, Martin Luther and many others. We also read more recent missionary stories.

Another example of how reading helped influence behavior came in the area of finances. When John and I were starting out, debt seemed like it was just a normal part of life. We did what everyone else we knew did: we bought a new car on payments, took out a significant mortgage for a new house, and were proud of all the credit cards we had been able to acquire. It was just what we thought you were supposed to do. However, our kids had a huge advantage over us.

Our children learned a different perspective about finances and debt. We had read several books about finances. *What Ever Happened to Penny Candy?* by Richard J. Maybury is a must-read book. Mayberry explains in concise, easy to understand language, the complicated subject of economics, finance, and investing. In Dave Ramsey's book, *Financial Peace*, we learned about budgeting and the history of debt in the United States. We were surprised to learn that the first credit card in the U.S. was the Diner's Club, issued in 1950. American Express was first issued in 1958, and Sears didn't have a credit card until it came out with the Discover Card in 1985. Currently, the credit card business itself has become a huge money-making industry (funded by the consumer). Before these cards were issued, most families had very little consumer debt. For most of America's history, debt was not a normal part of life. Other than a small mortgage, I don't think our grandparents had any debt. Our children also learned that the Scriptures warned that there were consequences to debt.

***The rich rules over the poor, And the borrower is servant to the lender. (Proverbs 22:7 (NKJV)***

We read biographies of faithful believers who believed God would provide everything they needed. These people trusted God, and although it was often difficult, God was always faithful. Stacie decided to trust God to provide for her college finances rather than taking out a student loan. This was radical thinking for this day and age, but we all prayed and supported her decision. It wasn't easy and often involved much personal sacrifice for her, but she believed this was what God wanted her to do. She applied for and received scholarships, worked part time, and we agreed to pay half of her undergraduate expenses. During her last semester, her finances were extremely tight so she decided to sell her car to pay the tuition. (The people who bought the car from her did all kinds of work to it and put many new parts in it, then sold it back to her. They charged her less than what they bought it from her for. Thank you, Kim and Kathy.) The car served her for many more years. Later, she gave it to her brother, who was sideswiped the first week he had it, and the car was totaled. He soon received an insurance payment for the car which was more money than Stacie had originally bought it for. God is so amazing. This story reminds me of the Israelites walking through the desert for forty years and their sandals never wearing out. She finished college debt free. God is faithful.

I can think of three additional specific examples of other blessings that unexpectedly came as a result of our reading with the children. As their world view and perspective grew:

1. They began to easily recognize propaganda.

2. They had a broader understanding of other forms of government.

3. They had a truer understanding of American history.

Many of the autobiographies we read told of firsthand accounts of living in other countries, during other time periods and under other forms of government. They began to appreciate and be grateful for the freedoms we have in America. They understood the cost of our freedom. We also read about real people in other societies and in other time periods being imprisoned or executed for disagreeing with a dictator, for reading the Scriptures, or for teaching their children to recite the Lord's Prayer. Their world view expanded and they also began to recognize the use of propaganda in different cultures and in our culture.

We see a good illustration of the use of propaganda in a delightful scene from the movie *The King and I*, (based on the memoirs of Anna Leonowens, governess to the children of King Mongkut of Siam.) In this scene, Anna (played by Deborah Kerr, the teacher for the children of the king, played by Yul Brynner) pulls down a map of the world. On the map, the country of Siam is front and center. Although in real life Siam (now Thailand) is a very small country, on the school map it encompasses a large portion of the world. The map depicts a picture of their king, who is large and strong carrying a massive sword next to a little, tiny, naked king of Burma in the country next to them running away from Siam's mighty king. Much to Anna's surprise, these bright-eyed children are to be taught that their country is the largest and most powerful country in the world. They are excited about learning and this is quite possibly the only source they have to learn from. They have no reason to believe it is not true. Although this is just a movie, this is an example of propaganda, and propaganda is very real. Anyone can become a victim of it.

According to the United States Memorial Museum Holocaust Encyclopedia, the Nazi's were adept at using propaganda.

> *Propaganda tries to force a doctrine on the whole people...*

> *"Propaganda works on the general public from the standpoint of an idea and makes them ripe for the victory of this idea." Adolf Hitler wrote these words in his book Mein Kampf (1926), in which he first advocated the use of propaganda to spread the ideals of National Socialism—among them racism, antisemitism and anti-Bolshevism.*

*Following the Nazi seizure of power in 1933, Hitler established a Reich Ministry of Public Enlightenment and Propaganda headed by Joseph Goebbels. The Ministry's aim was to ensure that the Nazi message was successfully communicated through art, music, theater, films, books, radio, educational materials, and the press.*

The Nazi's weren't alone in using propaganda to influence people. I just finished a book called *The Girl with Seven Names, Escape from North Korea,* by Hyeonseo Lee, about a young woman who escaped from North Korea. Her story is similar to the stories of others who have also escaped from there. She tells what she experienced growing up. Indoctrination began immediately. Her first day in kindergarten marked a shift from belonging to her parents to belonging to the state. Pictures on the wall included children playing games and having fun, as well as a North Korean soldier impaling a "Yankee", a Japanese, and a South Korean soldier all at the same time. The stories and songs were full of North Korean child heroes, and of boyhood stories about the how North Korean leader Kim Il-sung suffered to help those less fortunate than he by giving away his food and water and even his shoes. North Korea was portrayed as the most powerful and just nation on earth. The stories about Kim Il-sung were unending. The propaganda was constant. According to Hyeonseo, she was taught that:

*He (Kim Il-sung) was an invincible warrior who had defeated two great imperial powers in one lifetime-something that had never happened before in five thousand years of our history. He fought 100,000 battles against the Japanese in ten years – and that was before he'd even defeated the Yankees. He would travel for days without resting. He could appear simultaneously in the east and in the west. In his presence flowers bloomed and snow melted.*

*Even the toys we played with were used for our ideological education. If I built a train out of building blocks, the teacher would tell me that I could drive it to South Korea to drive the starving children home to the bosom of Respected Father Leader.* [4]

She had no reason to believe that she was taught lies, at least until she was much older and could see that reality didn't always align itself with what she had been taught. She later also learned that disagreeing with the government incurred severe consequences.

We'd like to believe this kind of thing could never happen in America because we are a free people. But can it happen here? While my children and I were studying Socialism in a history class, we compared two different school textbooks. One described Socialism as a positive, fair system of government where everyone is treated fairly, and the rich and poor all have equal access to all goods and services. The other textbook described facts about countries which had established this form of government. It detailed the suffering of the citizens. This second textbook presented a viewpoint that completely contradicted the first. Fortunately, our children had already had exposure to this system from reading biographies of people who had lived under this form of government and could think for themselves.

The children had read first-hand accounts of people waiting in long lines for inadequate amounts of food in socialist countries. While my daughter was having a conversation with a friend about a Socialist running for President in a recent election, I overheard her quote Margaret Thatcher's famous statement, "The problem with

---

[4] Lee, Hyeonseo, *The Girl with Seven Names, North Korean Defector's Story*, (Great Britain: William Collins, 2015), 22.

Socialism is that eventually you run out of other people's money." I was thankful for the reading we had done. She knew there was more to Socialism than "free stuff." The higher the percentage of taxes a central government takes from its people, the more the government uses this money to make choices for its citizens. The more choices the government makes for the people, the less freedom those citizens have to make their own choices. Our children possessed the tools needed in order to evaluate what they were learning in their classes and hearing on social media.

A third benefit from our reading is an understanding of American History.

Reading from original sources is a good safeguard against myths and revisionist history, and the misuse of phrases, such as "The Separation of Church and State." When we know true history, we can avoid making some of the same mistakes those who went before us made.

Although revisionists portray America's founders as atheists, agnostics and deists, it is not difficult at all to prove otherwise. The Founding Fathers of America implicitly stated that our rights were given to us by the Creator, not by men, not by the Cosmos and not by government:

> *We hold these truths to be self-evident: that all men are created equal; that they are endowed by their Creator with certain unalienable rights; that among these are life, liberty, and the pursuit of happiness.* (Declaration of Independence. Congress, July 4, 1776)

Our government was never meant to be void of religion. In a message to the Officers of the First Brigade of the Third Division of the Militia of Massachusetts, on October 11, 1798, John Adams (Second President of the United States) stated:

*Our Constitution was made only for a moral and religious people. It is wholly inadequate to the government of any other.*

By reading many of our Founding Fathers' writings and our country's documents, it becomes clear that our Founding Fathers were theists and predominately Christian. I highly recommend teaching our children to read some of the actual writings of those who founded America so they will not be deceived by much of what they hear about America's origins. (Also, teach them cursive writing so they are able to read the original documents, which are often written in cursive. Many elementary schools have stopped teaching children to write in cursive.) Many of the Founding Fathers' own words clearly demonstrate that most were Christian and that our nation was founded on Biblical principles from which true liberty and justice are derived. The following is just a small sample of some of our Founding Fathers' own words:

*I recommend my Soul to that Almighty Being who gave, and my body I commit to the dust, relying upon the merits of Jesus Christ for a pardon of all my sins.* From the will of Samuel Adams, Father of the American Revolution, Signer of the Declaration of Independence.

*To the eternal, immutable, and only true God be all honor and glory, now and forever, Amen!* From the will of Charles Cotesworth Pinckney, Signer of the Constitution

*Rendering thanks to my Creator for my existence and station among His works, for my birth in a country enlightened by the Gospel and enjoying freedom, and for all His other kindnesses, to Him I resign myself, humbly confiding in His goodness and in His mercy*

*through Jesus Christ for the events of eternity.* From the will of John Dickenson, Signer of the Constitution

*I, John Hancock...being advanced in years and being of perfect mind and memory --thanks be given to God-- therefore calling to mind the mortality of my body and knowing it is appointed for all men once to die [Hebrews 9:27], do make and ordain this my last will and testament...Principally and first of all, I give and recommend my soul into the hands of God that gave it: and my body I recommend to the earth...nothing doubting but at the general resurrection I shall receive the same again by the mercy and power of God.* From the will of John Hancock, signer of the Declaration of Independence.

*Unto Him who is the author and giver of all good, I render sincere and humble thanks for His manifold and unmerited blessings, and especially for our redemption and salvation by His beloved Son. He has been pleased to bless me with excellent parents, with a virtuous wife, and with worthy children. His protection has companied me through many eventful years, faithfully employed in the service of my country; His providence has not only conducted me to this tranquil situation, but also given me abundant reason to be contented and thankful. Blessed be His only name!* From the Will of John Jay, first Chief Justice of the Supreme Court.

Almost all of the fifty-five Founding Fathers who framed the Constitution were members of Christian churches, and over half of the signers of the Declaration of Independence received degrees from schools that today would be called Bible schools or seminaries,[5] and our Founding Fathers and even most of our Presidents recognized that our Nation was founded on the Bible and its principles. For example:

> *It [the Bible] is the rock on which our Republic rests.* President Andrew Jackson[6]

> *It was for the love of the Truths of this Great Book [the Bible] that our fathers abandoned their native shores for the wilderness. Animated by its lofty principles, they toiled and suffered till the desert blossomed as the rose [Isaiah 35:1] The Bible is the best of books and I wish it were in the hands of everyone. It is indispensable to the safety and permanence of our institutions; a free government cannot exist without religion and morals, and there cannot be morals without religion, nor religion without the Bible. Especially should the Bible be placed in the hands of the young. It is the best schoolbook in the world...I would that all of our people were brought up under the influence of that Holy Book.* President Zachary Taylor [7]

> *The Bible is the best gift God has given to men. All the good the Savior gave to the world was communicated*

---

[5] John Sergeant, Eulogy on Charles Carroll of Carrollton Delivered at the Request of the Select and Common Councils of the City of Philadelphia, December 31, 1832 (Philadelphia: Lydia R. Bailey, 1833), p.18.

[6] Ronald Reagan, "Proclamation 5018 – Year of the Bible, 1983," American Presidency Project.

[7] The President and the Bible," *New York Semi Weekly Tribune*, Wednesday, May 9, 1849, Vol. IV, no. 100, p. 1.

*through this book. But for it, we could not know right from wrong.* President Abraham Lincoln[8]

*The teachings of the Bible are so interwoven and entwined with our whole civic and social life that it would be literally-I do not mean figuratively, I mean literally- impossible for us to figure to ourselves what that life would be if these teaching were removed. We would lose almost all the standards by which we now judge both public and private morals.* President Teddy Roosevelt [9]

*America was born to exemplify that devotion to the elements of righteousness which are derived from the revelations of Holy Scripture.* President Woodrow Wilson [10]

*Of the many influences that that have shaped the United States of America into a distinctive Nation and people, none may be said to be more fundamental and enduring that the Bible.* President Ronald Reagan[11]

---

[8] Abraham Lincoln, *Abraham Lincoln Complete Works,* ed. John G. Nicolay and John Hay (New York: The Century Co., 1894), Vol. II, p. 574, "Reply to Committee of Colored People of Baltimore Who Presented Him with a Bible," Sept 7.1864.

[9] *Bible Society Record* (New York: The American Bible Society, 1901) Vol. 46, p. 99, Number 7, "Vice President Theodore Roosevelt Addresses the Long Island Bible Society."

[10] Woodrow Wilson, *The Papers of Woodrow Wilson*, ed. Arthur S. Link (Princeton, NJ: Princeton University Press, 1977), Vol. 23, p. 20, "An Address in Denver on the Bible," May 7, 1911.

[11] Ronald Reagan, "Proclamation 5018 – Year of the Bible, 1983," American Presidency Project.

The Founding Fathers built our government and Constitution on principles set forth in the Bible, and they understood that the further our nation drifted from these principles, the less strength we would have as a nation.

By reading books from our Founding Fathers' era, we can also easily understand the Founders' original intent pertaining to the role of religion and morality in the public arena, and how today's understanding of "separation of church and state" undermines their emphasis on religious freedom, which so many gave their lives to secure for us. Does "separation of church and state" mean that the government cannot be involved in anything that is religious? Does it mean a Nativity Scene cannot be put on government property? Does a football coach praying before a game in a public school violate "separation of church and state"? Is it "unconstitutional" to display the Ten Commandments in a courtroom? How do these kinds of issues compare with the Founders' writings and actions? Did the Founding Fathers prohibit everything religious from all government publications and property?

The Founding Fathers did not have any objection to religion and morality being promoted in the public square. In fact, the *New England Primer*, published first in 1690, was the book used to teach many of our Founding Fathers reading and Bible lessons. It was the first public school textbook printed in America. It would be absurd to believe those Founders would consider that such an important part of America's tradition would be considered unconstitutional because of its religious content. *The New England Primer* was the foundation of most colonial schooling before the 1790's. It is estimated that six to eight million copies had been sold by 1830 throughout colonial America. Its theme included the doctrine of original sin and of salvation through the death and resurrection of Jesus Christ. It also encompassed the foundations of Biblical Christianity. Consider this prayer the primer opens with:

## The Young Infant's or Child's Morning Prayer

*Almighty God the Maker of everything in Heaven and Earth; the Darkness goes away, and the Day light comes at thy Command. Thou art good and doest good continually.*

*I Thank thee that thou hast taken such Care of me this Night, and that I am alive and well this Morning.*

*Save me, O God, from Evil, all this Day long, and let me love and serve thee forever, for the Sake of Jesus Christ thy Son. Amen (New England Primer)*

## The Infant's or Young Child's Evening Prayer

*O LORD God who knowest all Things, thou seest me by Night as well as by Day.*

*I pray thee for Christ's Sake, forgive me whatever I have done amiss this Day, and keep me all this Night, while I am asleep.*

*I desire to lie down under thy Care, and to abide forever under the Blessing, for thou art a God of all Power and everlasting Mercy. Amen.* [12]

This small first grade reader goes on to teach children the alphabet, prayers, Bible Stories, the Ten Commandments, the Short Westminster Catechism, and a biblical world view. The Founding Fathers did not believe Religion and Morality should be separate

---

[12] Cotton, John, *The New England Primer*, (Boston: Edward Draper Printer 1777)

from government, education nor the civil arena. In fact, Congress approved the publishing of the first American Bible, the Aitken Bible, 1782.

> *RESOLVED, THAT the United States in Congress assembled highly approve the pious and laudable undertaking of Mr. Aitken, as subservient to the interest of religion, as well as an instance of the progress of arts in this country, and being satisfied from the above report of his care and accuracy in the execution of the work, they recommend this edition of the Bible to the inhabitants of the United States, and hereby authorize him to publish this Recommendation in the manner he shall think proper. Journals of the Continental Congress* [13]

Where did this phrase, "separation of church and state" come from? It is found nowhere in the Constitution. Neither does the phrase appear in any founding document. Although the phrase is often coupled with the First Amendment, this amendment does not forbid religion in the marketplace, school, government, or anywhere else in society. It simply states that Congress shall make no law respecting an establishment of religion or prohibiting the free exercise thereof.

Thirteen years after the First Amendment was written, the phrase "separation of church and state" had appeared in a letter written by Thomas Jefferson to the Baptists of Danbury, Connecticut assuring them that the government would not restrict their public expression of religious beliefs. Many Christian colonists who came to America

---

[13] *Washington: Government Printing Office, 1907, Vol. XIII, p. 574, September 12, 1782; The Holy Bible, Containing the Old and New Testaments (Philadelphia: Robert Aitken, 1782)*

had been subject to persecution from State leaders who had overtaken the Church. For example:

> *A decade after the Pilgrims settled at Plymouth, 20,000 Puritans also fled England after many received life sentences (or had their noses slit, ears cut off, or a brand placed on their foreheads) for not adhering to the State-mandated Anglican teachings. Others coming to America for similar reasons included Jews facing the Inquisition in Portugal (1654); Quakers fleeing England after some 10,000 had been imprisoned or tortured (1680); Anabaptists (Mennonites, Moravians, Dunkers, etc.) persecuted in Germany (1683); 400,000 Bible-Believing Huguenots persecuted in France (1685); and 20,000 Lutherans expelled from Austria (1731).*[14]

America was to be a place where people could practice their faith without persecution, regardless of their denomination. The letter from Thomas Jefferson containing the phrase "separation of church and state" was an assurance to the Baptists of Danbury that there would not be a state-run church. There would be a wall of separation, protecting the church from the power of the state. The Constitution protected freedom of conscience, which is the freedom to live out our belief in the public square without interference from the government. It restricted only the government. There were no restrictions on people to practice their faith anywhere or anytime.

When the original meaning of the "wall of separation" was challenged by some who wanted to restrict freedom of religion in the public square, it was struck down immediately by the Supreme Court. In the Supreme Court Case, *Reynolds v. U.S. (1878),* the

---

[14] The Founders' Bible NAS, 1st Ed. Gen. Eds. Bob Cummings and Lance Wubbels. (California; Shiloh Road Publishers, 2012): 686

plaintiffs tried using the term "separation of church and state" to restrict religious activity in the public arena.

> *The Supreme Court responded not by merely citing Jefferson's metaphor (which is all that most courts today do) but rather by reprinting a lengthy segment from his letter to prove that "separation of church and state" was to preserve rather than remove Christian values and practices in public policy.*[15]

The understanding of the protection of religion from government was maintained in the courts until 1947. A radical change occurred in the Supreme Court case *Everson v. Board of Education, 1947*. Only the words "separation of church and state" were cited in the case. The context and the rest of the letter were ignored, and a new standard was constructed.

> *The First Amendment has erected a wall between church and state. That wall must be kept high and impregnable. We could not approve the slightest breach.* [16]

As a result of the decision, almost two centuries of protection for public religious expression was undermined and reversed. The court misused a single expression from a private letter and reversed the original intent of the First Amendment. This ruling influenced subsequent religious freedom cases and eroded the freedom to practice our faith.

Our Founding Fathers knew and warned us that citizens must stay educated and active in this government of the people, by the people, and for the people. If we do not remain educated and active, our freedoms, secured by the sacrifice of so many, will be taken from us.

---

[15] Reynolds v. U.S., 98 U.S. 145, 164 (1878)
[16] Everson v. Board of Education, 330 U.S. 1, 18 (1947)

This is clearly demonstrated by the myth of the "separation of state" issue. Many citizens do not understand our history and the value religion and morality played in forming America. Many believe religion has no place in the public arena. This simply is not true and reading American history from original sources proves it. We can encourage our children to read and understand the truth and to live accordingly.

When we began reading to our children, I never dreamed there would be so many benefits. In the time it would have taken our family to watch one or two television programs per evening, we were able to dramatically enrich our children's lives. Their reading comprehension was enhanced, vocabulary enlarged, and their world view expanded. They learned to understand other people and other cultures, and they learned some financial management skills. They have a better understanding of American history, and they have some tools to protect themselves from much of the propaganda that surrounds them. But even more important, we all cherish those evenings from those many years that passed so quickly. Those priceless memories live on in each one of our hearts.

*Kitty Spencer*

# Chapter 7

## *Managing Everyday Finances*

When my husband and I got married, we knew very little about financial management. We looked around, saw what everyone else was doing, and did likewise. We bought a new house and new cars on credit, just as all of our friends had done. We figured if we could qualify for loans for these things, we could afford them. It all seemed normal. Neither of us had ever taken any kind of financial planning class, and we didn't realize that being able to qualify for a loan and actually being able to afford the loan can be two entirely different things. The house payment and the car payments did not leave a lot of financial margin in our life. Then, while still living in Phoenix, adding a couple of children to the family made our finances even tighter. We next decided that I should quit my job and stay home with the kids, and that added even more stress to our financial situation.

Staying home with the children was a tough decision for us, but we began to realize that most of the income I was making was going into childcare, gasoline, work clothes, and eating out more often because many times I was just too tired to cook. Also, I wanted to give my best to my family, but after work there wasn't much left to give. They got my leftovers, which usually meant fatigue and grouchiness. I know other people may have enough energy to work outside the home and still take good care of their families, but I am not one of them. As we prayed about the situation, God confirmed my decision in His Word. Titus 2:2-4 admonishes older women to teach younger women to, among other things, be keepers of the home. This was a clear command to me from God. I was to be a keeper of the home, and I wanted to do it well. The will of God is often hard to discern, but this is something He made very clear to me. I decided to make it a priority and do my best at keeping my home in order. Then with any extra time and energy I had, I could pursue other things. I found that caring for my family and home, and giving adequate time and effort to my spiritual life was about all I could manage at that time. I had to give up my medical career.

On top of loss of income from quitting my job, we had some unexpected medical bills and growing credit card debt to add to our car payments and mortgage. It became more and more difficult to make ends meet. Finally, that defining moment came when we knew we had to make some changes.

It began on one miserably hot, sunny afternoon while we were walking through the mall. (That's just what we did to escape the scorching Phoenix summer sun.) We wandered into Sears where my husband saw a cordless drill and decided he wanted it. I looked at him and he looked at me. I shook my head no and asked,

"You don't get it, do you?"

"Get what?" he asked, having no idea what I was talking about and probably thinking *this is another one of those I just don't understand women moments.*

I responded with, "You REALLY don't get it, do you?"

Again, he asked, "Get WHAT?"

I calmly answered, "We absolutely cannot afford this!"

With a confused look on his face, he asked, "What do you mean, we can't afford this? I work hard all week and this doesn't cost that much."

I left the mall with a disgruntled husband, with no drill, and with a lot of work to do on our finances.

I'd been paying most of the bills without my husband's involvement, and after paying bills, the checking account always hovered around zero. He was becoming resentful of not having enough money to buy what he thought he should have, and I couldn't seem to figure out where the money was going. It just seemed to slip between our fingers, never to appear again. It was becoming easier and easier to buy things on a credit card, and I knew that was not a good idea. Our finances were crumbling before our eyes. We decided to work on this problem together. We sat down over some iced tea and looked over our money situation. We realized we had an unbelievable financial disaster on our hands. Something had to change.

Our situation reminded me of a story I came across during my Bible reading time. In 2 Kings 19, Hezekiah, King of Judah, was in a treacherous situation with no escape. The Assyrians had been conquering nation after nation around him. He received a letter from Sennacherib, King of Assyria, stating that Sennacherib's armies were going to destroy Judah, Hezekiah's nation, as well. Assyria's army was far superior militarily to Judah's and everyone knew it. They were about to be slaughtered by this fierce nation. (Now admittedly, we weren't nearly in as bad a situation as Hezekiah was, but we were in financial trouble, and just as Hezekiah couldn't see any possible solution to his trouble, we couldn't see any possible solution to our trouble.) So what did Hezekiah do?

> *Hezekiah took the letter from the envoy and read it. He went to The Temple of GOD and spread it out before GOD. And Hezekiah prayed—oh, how he prayed! GOD, God of Israel, seated in majesty on the cherubim-throne. You are the one and only God, sovereign over all kingdoms on earth, Maker of heaven, maker of earth. Open your ears, GOD, and listen, open your eyes and look. Look at this*

*letter Sennacherib has sent, a brazen insult to the living God! The facts are true, O GOD: The kings of Assyria have laid waste countries and kingdoms. Huge bonfires they made of their gods, their no-gods hand-made from wood and stone. But now O GOD, our God, save us from raw Assyrian power; Make all the kingdoms on earth know that you are GOD, the one and only God. (2 Kings 19:14–19, The Message)*

God answered Hezekiah's prayer. God prevented Sennacherib, King of Assyria, from conquering Hezekiah and his people!

*And it so happened that that very night an angel of GOD came and massacred 185,000 Assyrians. When the people of Jerusalem got up next morning, there it was—a whole camp of corpses! (2 Kings 19:34–35, The Message)*

I know, that's somewhat gory, but God did answer. Just as Hezekiah spread out the letter from Sennacherib before God, we spread our financial situation before God and prayed. God is sovereign over all the earth. He is the Maker of Heaven and earth. Just as Hezekiah acknowledged that the facts were true, we acknowledged our facts were true. Our finances were disastrous and we couldn't see any way out. But God answered our prayer, too, step by step. He showed us how to work through our financial crisis. He directed our path.

*Trust in the LORD with all your heart, and lean not on your own understanding; In all your ways acknowledge Him, And He shall direct your paths. (Proverbs 3:5–6, NKJV)*

The first thing we did was sign up for a financial seminar being offered at a local church. We went and felt totally overwhelmed. It covered a lot more information than we could possibly digest in one weekend, so we focused on two aspects of the weekend. We concentrated on stewardship and monthly budgeting. With calculator in hand and plenty of paper on the table, we began.

We had been tithing, but the concept of stewardship was new to us. We, like many other believers just thought that we needed to pay our tithe and the rest of our money was ours to spend as we pleased. Not so, according to God's Word.

> *The earth is the LORD's, and all its fullness, the world and those who dwell therein. (Psalm 24:1, NKJV)*

Everything is the Lord's, including all of our resources. He is not just interested in the percentage we give to Him, but in everything we have. We are stewards of God's resources. The dictionary definition of a steward is: "A person who manages another's property or financial affairs." Financial faithfulness ultimately flows out of the recognition that everything we are and everything we have belongs to the Lord.

> *To you, O God, belong the greatness and the might, the glory, the victory, the majesty, the splendor; Yes! Everything in heaven, everything on earth; the kingdom all yours! You've raised yourself high over all. Riches and glory come from you, you're ruler over all; You hold strength and power in the palm of your hand to build up and strengthen all. And here we are, O God, our God, giving thanks to you, praising your splendid Name. But me—who am I, and who are these my people, that we should presume to be giving something to you? Everything comes from you; all we're doing is giving back what we've been given from your generous hand. As far as you're concerned, we're homeless, shiftless wanderers like our ancestors, our lives mere shadows, hardly anything to us. God, our God, all these materials— these piles of stuff for building a house of worship for you, honoring your Holy Name—it all came from you! It*

*was all yours in the first place! (1 Chronicles 29:11–16, The Message)*

Everything we have belongs to God. We might wonder, "Why should we even care about how we manage our money?" Or "Does it really matter to God?" I think the answer to those questions come from the words of Jesus, Himself:

*One who is faithful in a very little is also faithful in much, and one who is dishonest in a very little is also dishonest in much. If then you have not been faithful in the unrighteous wealth, who will entrust to you the true riches? (Luke 16:10–11, ESV)*

We are managers for God of the resources He has entrusted to us. He cares about how we use all of those resources. He cares about us. He cares about where we live. He cares about what we eat and what we wear. He understands our need for transportation and technology and everything else. We decided to partner with the Lord in ALL of our financial decisions from that time forward. Becoming wise and prudent with our finances helps us to not let resources slip through our fingers on unnecessary spending and waste, and it helps us to have resources to help with our needs and needs around us and around the world. A faithful steward is one who exercises discipline, wisdom, skill and prudence in the management of God's resources. It was time for us to work on becoming faithful stewards.

Faithful stewards also pursue unity in marriage. Financial discord often destroys marriages. Financial problems are one of the major causes for divorce.

John and I had work to do. We had very different attitudes toward spending money. We both came from frugal families, but John, although careful with finances, liked very nice things of good quality and reliability. I, on the other hand, wanted to save money and to always get by as cheaply as possible. I lived by the old depression era motto, "Use it up, wear it out; make it last or do without." John went by his own motto, "You get what you pay for. Don't buy junk." I noticed this difference soon after we became engaged.

I had been driving an old 1965 Ford Falcon, and I had mastered the ritual needed in order to get the car started. First I would turn the key in the ignition, and it often would not crank the engine over. If it did not start, I would turn the key off, get out of the car, lift the hood, jiggle the battery wires, close everything up, get back into the car, and try again. Then it would usually start. If not, I would try again. My dad had taught me well, and I was pretty proud of my auto mechanic prowess. This had been going on for several months, and I didn't think anything was weird about it, and I was saving money.

One time, John was riding with me. The car did not start, so I began my routine. After the car started, he suggested we go to an auto parts store (our first of many auto-store dates). I agreed, although I didn't think that it was necessary. He bought me a battery ground wire assembly and installed it. The car started immediately, and I no longer had to perform my battery wire shaking ritual. It had never before crossed my mind before John replaced the battery wire that you could buy a new part. I had learned a lot from my dad, and making do with car problems was one of those things. Bailing wire and duct tape were his specialty, and I was a good student who learned this well. After this lesson with John, I realized that maybe there were other ways to do things than the way I had always seen them done. For example, I was surprise when John wanted to buy Dawn dish soap, and not Palmolive. Dawn was fine, but I had always bought Palmolive and had never even though of buying a different brand.

I was a saver, and John was a spender. This eventually led to conflict and a constant source of stress. We knew that setting up a spending plan would help. We began setting up the plan we had learned about at the financial seminar. Wise stewards learn to work together and having a spending plan is vital to working together. To set up our plan, we used material from Larry Burkett, a well-known

Christian author and financial counselor. We didn't do everything right, but we worked at it. By using his envelope budgeting system, we took our first steps on our journey to financial freedom.

The envelope budgeting plan we chose, like most of the other budgeting plans available, follow the same basic, principles: First, you determine how much income you bring home each month. (If your income isn't stable, you take a monthly income average from the previous year.) Next, you determine what you have been spending each month. This may take a while. Different budgeting programs will give specific instructions on how to do this. Some have you track every cent you spend for a period of time; others have you look at your records to determine your spending. Spending is then divided into various categories such as: Giving, Transportation, Housing, Food, Clothing, Medical, Insurance, Savings, etc. You allocate a dollar amount into each category, based on what you have determined you have been spending each month. Next, you add up the total spending categories, including a savings category, and compare it to your income for each month. The goal was to have the total dollar amount from each spending category equal the dollar amount of income for each month.

As we were beginning our budget using the Burkett envelope system, we soon recognized our spending exceeded our income. This is not an uncommon revelation when first trying to get a spending plan on paper. Our next step was to lay out each budget category, one by one, before the Lord, and ask Him to show us what changes, if any, needed to be made in that category.

Our first category was giving. We both believed our first commitment was giving to the Lord. Honoring God with our giving is one of our core values. God wants us to be conduits of His blessings. He uses our giving to help those in need. I am convinced that God can make the ninety percent leftover after tithing go farther than one hundred percent if we don't tithe. We have seen that happen time and time again. We continued tithing.

Our next category was housing. Most budgeting programs we have studied recommend keeping the cost of housing, including mortgage or rent, utilities, technology, and repairs below 40 percent of the total take home pay. Anything greater than 40 percent puts a family under financial pressure and adds considerable stress to the household. Downsizing is sometimes the preferable option when finances are out of control and the mortgage or rent is swallowing up too much of the family income. Our housing expenses were a little more than the forty percent, but getting a smaller house would not have saved us any money. Prices had risen so significantly since we bought this house, it was unlikely we would be able to buy or rent anything cheaper. We kept the house in our new budget we were creating. We were able to save a little on our homeowner's insurance by comparing prices from various insurance companies and by raising our deductible. We didn't have cell phones and we did survive. We changed the temperature a few degrees on the house thermostat to save a little more, and also started wearing our clothes more than once before washing them. These were just little things, but they were a launching point for us becoming more frugal (some would say cheap).

The area we definitely needed to make some changes in was transportation. The car payments were a huge strain on the cash flow. It was convenient for us to have two cars, but we knew we could get by on one. I could drive my husband to work and use the car if I needed it, or he could drive to work and I could just run errands after he got home. It meant sacrifice and it was a hard choice, but as we prayed about it, we agreed it was a wise plan. Selling the car and eliminating a car payment took an unbelievable amount of stress out of our lives. We were so relieved to not have the financial stress of the car payment, and having only one car wasn't really that bad. It turned out we had made a great decision. Then, out of nowhere, we got an unexpected blessing. Someone gave us a car. I believe the Lord blessed our feeble attempts of honoring Him with our finances.

Food was a category that I had never been able to manage well. Every couple of weeks I would go to the refrigerator and throw out bunches of wasted leftovers. Now, many years later, I think I am beginning to make some improvements. My grandmother was my role model for eating well and not wasting food, and I think about her every time I load the garbage disposal with wasted leftovers, and vow I will do better next time. I have found that making a menu and grocery list and sticking to the list really helps. Also, eating leftovers before cooking a new dish and avoiding extra trips to the grocery store both help the food budget.

We continued prayerfully considering each budget category and made reasonable changes accordingly. We were finally able to balance our monthly expenditures with our income.

Here is a list for some general guidelines for setting up budget categories:

| | | |
|---|---|---|
| 1. | Giving | 10% or more |
| 2. | Savings | 5% or more |
| 3. | Housing | 40% or less |
| 4. | Medical | 5% |
| 5. | Transportation | 10% |
| 6. | Debt Repayment | 5% |
| 7. | Recreation | 2% to 5% |
| 8. | Personal allowance | 1% to 5% |
| 9. | Food | 10% to 20% |
| 10. | Insurance | 1% to 5% |
| 11. | Clothing | 5% to 7% |
| 12. | Miscellaneous | 1% to 5% |

These are not set in stone, but can give you a general idea of what reasonable category percentages might look like. After you have finished adjusting the budget amounts, the total combined percentages from each category must add up to 100%. Each time we got paid, we withdrew cash and filled our budget category envelopes with the predetermined dollar amount and spent from the envelopes. When the envelopes were empty, we couldn't spend from that category until it was refilled. If there was leftover cash in the envelope, we kept the leftover amount in the envelope and had that much more available for the next pay period.

For the first time in my life, I began to feel financial freedom. I could buy something without feeling guilty about it. No guilt! It was amazing. We also set aside a portion for each of us for an allowance. We could spend it on anything we wanted. We didn't have to justify a need in order to buy something. This was new for me. I could buy something just for fun. I cannot explain the freedom I felt. John was also free within the boundaries we set to shop all he wanted in order to find good quality items. If he wanted something that cost more than we had, we just had to wait a little while until there was more saved up. He really started to feel free, too. He no longer had to worry at all about me throwing a fit because I thought he spent too much on something. This whole money plan felt like a gift from God to us.

Finances were still extremely tight, but we were consistently chipping away at our debt, and no longer borrowing. A job opportunity opened up for us in Washington, and through much prayer (and tears - mine) we believed God was directing us to move. John decided to apply for the job, and he got it. Three weeks later we were in Washington, and John was working as a contractor for Boeing. The job paid quite a bit more than his previous job and our spending plan wasn't as tight. We continued to use our newly learned financial management skills. We also took more classes in order to sharpen these skills, and eventually began teaching budgeting classes to others who also struggled in this area.

We did not want our children to make the financial mistakes we made, so we came up with a plan for training them about finances. Although we weren't always very good at following through with the plan to train them, we tried. When they began understanding the concept of money, we provided them with three jars – one for tithing, one for saving, and one for spending. Every time they received money, we helped them put ten percent in the tithing jar, ten percent in the savings jar, and the rest in the spending jar. They took pleasure in bringing their tithe to church and putting it in the offering. They also liked watching their savings grow. The money in the spending jar could be used at their discretion. This money was for them to buy things they just wanted to have. This helped them to understand how to make decisions and understand that once you spent cash on something it was spent, and no longer available. If they wanted something different, they would have to wait until they had more money. The savings was meant for some larger purchase, something they really wanted, but would take months to save for. (For Keith, it was usually a large Lego ™ set.) We wanted them to understand delayed gratification.

As the kids grew older, we gave them more responsibility over their finances. For instance, we gave them a clothing envelope to save for school shopping. There wasn't a lot of cash, but there was enough to buy the clothes they needed. One time, one of them went to the second hand store and bought several really nice outfits with the clothing money. The other (I won't say which one) went to a fancy store and bought a name brand pair of shoes. I think the second child was a little bit sorry for the choice made upon seeing the other's loot.

We didn't always stick to the budget, and we were way too soft hearted when it came to buying things for the kids. Actually, we loved to get them things and loved to bless them, just like I know our heavenly Father blesses us so abundantly. We were concerned, however, that if we gave them too much, they would develop a dangerous entitlement mentality and not really learn the value of money. Even I, the parent, was really surprised how easily I slipped into expecting free things from others.

We had gone to the fair. I was having a lot of pain in my feet and was using a wheelchair at that time. John pushed me up to the gate to purchase tickets, fully expecting to pay the full entrance fee. The person selling tickets said we both could get in free because of the handicap. I was so thankful and felt really surprised and blessed. We went to another fair a few months later. Again, we went to the gate to pay. This time my expectations were different. I hoped and half expected that maybe we would get in free again. This time, however, we were both charged the full fee. I was disappointed and actually felt a little anger creep up inside me. Didn't they even care about my poor little feet? My response to the entire situation floored me. I couldn't believe I was feeling that way. Really! Why should I expect to get in free? I certainly didn't expect to get in for free during the previous visit to the fair. I recognized how easy it is to feel entitled, and I didn't want my kids to ever feel like that. Fortunately, thanks to God's grace, they didn't seem to develop bad attitudes and they remained thankful for gifts we gave them.

When our son was about fifteen, we decided to make sure he was more prepared than we were to venture into the big, confusing dog eat dog financial world out there. We were rummaging through a Christian bookstore when we found a little book called *Creating Your Own Personal Money MAP* by Ethan Pope. There are several resources to learn about budgeting by various authors such as Larry Burkett, Dave Ramsey, Ron Blue, and many others. These are easily found with an internet search. Almost all of them are fundamentally the same. The one we found looked simple and straight forward and appropriate for a fifteen-year-old. We asked our son and his friend Stephen if they wanted to work through this book with us. They said, "Sure," so we set up a time to meet with them once a week for several weeks to work on it. After studying this book with our son and his friend, we decided to switch our own financial management to the MAP (Money Allocation Plan) described in it. It was essentially the same as the envelope plan, except we kept track of the money balances in categories on paper rather than using actual envelopes and cash. We were able help the boys set up a monthly money spending plan, and we all learned more about how to set up life-long goals.

I am happy to report that after many years of watching Keith make both good and bad financial decisions, we are now seeing genuine fruit from the time we spent training him on budgeting and goal setting.

Setting up life-long financial goals can be confusing. People often wonder whether to pay off credit cards first or put money into a 401K plan. Should I pay extra on the house payment or the car payment? Do I support God's Kingdom or pay off debts first, then begin giving? Trying to plan for an emergency, retirement, IRA, kid's college, debt repayment, and car savings can be overwhelming. We want to do all of these things, but if we try to do them all at once, we often make very little progress, get discouraged, feel as if we are spinning our wheels and just give up.

This part of our budgeting really confused us for years. We kept trying to pay for all these things and never could make much progress. Finally, while reading the Ethan Pope money MAP book, the lights came on and we understood we didn't have to try to pay all these things at once. We could set up a plan to do these things one at a time.

Dave Ramsey uses the term "baby steps" to describe how to accomplish all of these goals. The term came from the comedy *What About Bob,* which was a movie about a very needy guy, (played by Bill Murray) who drives his psychiatrist, (played by Richard Dreyfus) crazy. The therapist finally tells him he can get anywhere if he takes one step at a time: baby steps. Dave Ramsey says you can achieve financial freedom if you take one small step at a time, hence the term, "baby steps." Crown Financial Ministries has a similar plan they call a "roadmap to financial freedom." In the book we use, Ethan Pope calls it "establishing your priorities."

Whether you call it "baby steps," "money MAP to financial freedom", "establishing your priorities," or something different, all of these organizations have worked with thousands of people and have shown that setting up these steps in your financial plan work well. Here is an example of how the plans generally work.

> ***Step 1.*** *First make the minimum payments on your mortgage, bills and debts, (we included tithe in this step.) Next, take any additional funding you have and concentrate on paying each of the following steps, one at a time. As each step is completed, take the income used for a completed step, and use it toward the next step.*

> ***Step 2:*** *Establish an emergency fund. At this step, start with $500 or 3% of your annual income, whichever is greater. (You will increase this emergency fund to 6 months take home pay in step 5.)*

> ***Step 3:*** *Eliminate credit card debt and other consumer debt. Make all minimum payment. Next, pay extra on the smallest debt until that is paid for. When the smallest one is paid off, add the amount you were paying on the smallest debt, to the next smallest debt. Continue this system, known as the snowball effect, to each debt until they are all paid off.*

> ***Step 4:*** *Pay off your car debt with extra money left over each month from not having to pay the credit card companies. After the car has been paid for, begin saving some of the funds you had been using for your car*

*payment to save for your next car. Use the rest of it for step five. The plan is to be able to pay cash for your next car.*

***Step 5:*** *Expand your emergency reserve fund to equal 6 month's take home pay.*

***Step 6:*** *Begin your long-term savings/investment plan. (Many financial planners recommend beginning a 401K plan as step 2, saving up to the amount the employer matches because this is a good source of basically free money. This works well, too.)*

***Step 7:*** *Pay off your mortgage. Become 100% debt free.*

***Step 8:*** *Give more freely to God's work and to other causes you have a passion for.*

Following these basic steps allows you to pay off debt and save for the future in an orderly, well-planned manner. This enables you to concentrate any funds not needed for immediate living expenses on your future priorities. It prevents you from squandering those funds for things that you may think you want at the moment, and using them on things you know that you will need later.

Preparing our children to manage finances is an important part of preparing them to leave the nest. If we don't teach them about money management, they are likely to fall into the financial problems so common in our society, where buying beyond our means is just expected and squandering money is normal. This often leads to marital discord. It is very common for money to slip through our fingers on frivolous, unimportant impulse items. Often, kids look around at the possessions others have or their parents have after many years of saving, and think borrowing is the way to have those things. It is easy and convenient, but not wise, and the consequences of debt can be devastating on a young family. Be proactive with your kids. You can begin teaching them when they are young to put any money they get into the saving, giving, and spending jars. As they grow older, they can learn more and more about financial management. Sometime before they leave home, teach them to budget, live within their means, and save for the future. After all the training, pray they actually put what they learned into practice.

# Chapter 8

# Relationships

I had a fairly simple childhood. Most families I knew consisted of a mother, father and children. Some couples had grown children, and a small number did not have any children. Growing up, all of my friends had moms and dads. I was twelve the first time I heard the term "single mom." It was in reference to my friend JoAnne's mom, after her dad died. Perhaps I grew up overprotected in a little social bubble.

I knew almost nothing about dating and relationships, even well into high school. I will admit right up front that I am not qualified to give advice about dating. For me, dating was a non-issue. When I was in high school, I stayed very busy with school work, drama, music and a group of wonderful friends. We did a lot together as a group, but never really paired off as boyfriends and girlfriends. At one point in my senior year, one of my close friends, David, asked me if I would be his back-up date in case the girl he was going to ask to the prom turned him down. I said I would. She said "No," so I went with him to the prom. Neither of us had any romantic interest in the other. We were just buddies. In college, I went out a couple of times, then I met John and we became best friends, and later, we got married. That is my entire dating-life in a nutshell. I had no residual heartaches from relationships gone sour. I credit much of this to a grandmother who prayed daily for me, and I think God protected me in my ignorance from relationships that could have gone bad.

I was about as naïve as anyone could have been about relationships and sex. I remember sitting in a health class in high school when the subject of sexually transmitted diseases was introduced. There was an overhead (remember those?) presenting a diagram of person A with lines connecting to each of five other people, labeled B, C, D, E, and F. Each of these five was connected to five more, like branches on a tree. The point of the diagram was to show that if person A had a sexually transmitted disease, and if person A had sexual relations with B, C, D, E, and/or F, those people would be exposed and could pass the disease to each of the many people they had sexual relationships with. I left the class completely confused. Silly me! I thought sex was only supposed to be within the confines of marriage. I think my grandmother had mentioned that once, and I had accepted it. I left class wondering if I had it all wrong, and I really didn't have anyone to ask. These things were not discussed in my home. Maybe sex was just something casual and maybe it was normal to sleep with several people. Fortunately, after John and I became good friends and I began to take the Bible seriously, we began reading Christian books and listening to speakers who taught from the Word of God on the subject, and I began to understand what God had said before I made poor choices. For the Christ follower, the answer is very clear and simple. God again tells us in His Word that sex is good and right only in the context of marriage. Period.

*Nevertheless, to avoid fornication, let every man have his own wife, and let every woman have her own husband. (1 Corinthians 7:2, KJV 1900)*

*Flee fornication. Every sin that a man doeth is without the body; but he that committeth fornication sinneth against his own body. (1 Corinthians 6:18, KJV 1900)*

*For from within, out of the heart of men, proceed evil thoughts, adulteries, fornications, murders. (Mark 7:21, KJV 1900)*

According to the *Collins English Dictionary,* the definition of fornication is voluntary sexual intercourse outside marriage. Many will argue that there is no problem with sex outside of marriage, as long as the two people are consenting and love each other. God's Word differs. God created us and knows what is best for us. He wants us to believe Him and trust Him. You don't have to look very far to see the destruction caused by the sexual revolution.

After we had children, and as they got older, we decided to address these issues with them. I did not want our kids to be as ignorant as I was about intimacy and I wanted them to have a Biblical view of marriage. When they reached their pre-teen years, I heard an episode on the popular radio show *Focus on the Family* with James Dobson. A six-part series designed to teach pre-teens Biblical principles on how to prepare for a healthy marriage was discussed. Cassette tape teachings on the subject were offered, so we decided to buy the cassette tape series (and an extra cassette player) and take our kids on a special getaway weekend to listen to the tapes. We got two rooms at a little bungalow in the woods, one for Keith and John, and one for Stacie and me.

We tried to make it a really special, exciting and fun weekend. John would listen to one of the sessions with Keith in their room while Stacie and I listened to a session in our room. We would discuss the session and answer any questions they had, then all four of us would meet together to do something fun like go out for ice-cream, go for a hike, or watch a movie. Afterwards, we would go to our respective rooms to hear the next session and answer questions, and so forth until we heard all six lessons. They learned incredible information, and I felt they were receiving a good foundation to prepare them for the teenage years that were to follow, and eventually for marriage. I believed they had some good tools to avoid many pitfalls that could await them.

The most prominent take-a-way from the weekend was an amazing, profound and clear verse from the book of Song of Solomon.

> *Young women of Jerusalem, I charge you by the gazelles and the wild does of the field: do not stir up or awaken love until the appropriate time. (Song of Solomon 3:5, HCSB)*

What does it mean to stir up or awaken love, and when is the appropriate time to do so? Stirring up love is a process of awakening passion in someone. Awakening passion can be illustrated in the example of a young couple experiencing what is often called the *law of diminishing returns.* The first time they feel an interest in each other, they might feel a slight surge of delight when one brushes up against the other. The next time they brush up against the other, they don't feel the delight as much, so they try something new. This time, perhaps, they hold hands and the sensation returns. This works for a while, but soon it takes more to get this feeling. A hand on the shoulder works for a while, then soon the feelings diminish, and it takes a hand on the waist to elicit the desire response. After a while, this is no longer as exciting so they move on to the next step. They try maybe hand to face, then face to face in a kiss, and then farther and farther until intimacy is achieved. This entire process is normal and created by God in the courting and marriage process. There is a time and a place for it. Sexual passion can be one of the strongest forces in human nature and is an important and valuable part of life. However, it can be dangerous. It is often compared to fire, and like fire, must be treated with respect and caution.

To move the analogy further, a fire in a fireplace can be a wonderful thing. However, a fire out of control that is not contained can be a disaster. The same is true of passion. Passion is wonderful when it remains where it belongs, in marriage, but can be a disaster when it is not controlled.

John and I saw first-hand what can happen when a fire gets out of control. We walked through what remained of my dad's home in Overgaard, Arizona after the *Rodeo-Chediski Fire* of 2002 had devastated over 460,000 acres of East Central Arizona. His concrete front steps stood alone in front of what used to be my dad's home. A large, mangled ash heap was all that remained of the house. A few charred trees dotted the property and off to the side was my dad's Gold-Wing motorcycle. It looked like the fire had missed it, but we later learned that all the tubes and wires had been melted by the intense heat from the fire. Similarly, this can happen when human passion is misdirected. In some kids, their emotions can resemble a mangled ash heap full of pain and despair after a misplaced relationship. In other kids, like the motorcycle, the damage is not quite as apparent. It is not uncommon for a boy or girl who appears to be fine after a break-up to really be damaged and broken-hearted for months or years after a break-up, or a series of break-ups.

A few years after the *Focus on the Family* cassette teaching weekend, we and the kids had the opportunity to volunteer for and attend a *Life on the Edge* conference which re-enforced the previous lessons they learned about relationships and preparation for marriage. Our kids understood that passion, marriage and sex are wonderful, but they also understood that it made absolutely no sense to stir up the passion before they were at a stage in life when they were prepared to be married. They understood dating could awaken feelings inside them that they should not pursue for years, until they were older and married. They both chose not to date until they were ready to consider marriage. I believe that part of the reason they were able to make the choice not to date was because they didn't experience peer pressure in this area. They were home educated and weren't around other young people that dated. Most of their close friends were interested in the projects and activities they were involved in, and didn't involve themselves in the whole dating scene.

It is important for kids to have a variety of friendships, and dating can get in the way of friendships. Dating seems to skip the friendship stage in a relationship because feelings can become consuming and couples often become very self-focused. A couple will often ignore other friendships while dating. Romance can bring euphoria, and everything else seems to fade into the background. All of a sudden, this feeling becomes the most important thing in their lives, and nothing else matters much. We did not want this to happen to our kids.

Adolescence is a time of when bodies grow and change quickly, and hormones bring heightened emotions. It can be a tumultuous time, but it is also a precious time in life. During this time, they do not have the responsibilities of life they will have when they are adults, and they are much more capable than they were as children. This is a time they can prepare themselves, learn, and grow. Their brains are like little sponges, and it is an absolute waste to spend this season of opportunity pining over who likes them and who doesn't.

During the Colonial period of our country, expectations were different than they are now. I often hear adults discussing ways to provide opportunities to help youths stay out of trouble. "If we only had skate parks or game rooms or youth groups that are more fun, we could keep these kids off the streets." I don't think this is what these teenagers really need. I believe they should be challenged to explore the gifts and talents the Lord had given them and develop these to the best of their ability. I believe they have great potential. Our founders provide examples of this kind of potential.

*When John Quincy Adams was eight years old, he performed musket drills during the Revolution with the famous Massachusetts Minutemen; when he was eleven, he received a congressional diplomatic appointment overseas as Secretary to the Ambassador in Paris and at age fourteen received a similar appointment to the Court of Catherine the Great in Russia.* [17]

*When Constitution signer William Livingston was fourteen, he moved in among the Mohawk Indians as a missionary.* [18]

*James Iredell – a Justice placed on the Supreme Court by George Washington – was appointed to pubic office in North Carolina to oversee financial matters when he was just seventeen years old.* [19]

*Andrew Jackson (who later became a U. S. President) was serving as a soldier in the American Revolution when only fourteen years old; he was captured and made a prisoner of war by the British.* [20]

Much was expected from children by the time they reached their early adolescent years. For those students who were going to continue their education at the University, it was not unusual for them to enter at the age of thirteen or fourteen. Others began apprenticeships at this age and began preparing for their careers under the tutelage of a master craftsman such as a tanner, shoemaker, tailor, watchmaker, silversmith, spinner, knitter, weaver or another.

We wanted to help our kids make the most out of these special years between childhood and adulthood. Scripture says to *"Train up a child in the way he should go; even when he is old he will not depart from it."* (Proverbs 22:6, ESV). As we studied this verse, we found that a child was designed with a certain bent, or direction that

---

[17] *Dictionary of American Biography*, s.v. "Adams, John Quincy."

[18] *Dictionary of American Biography*, s.v. "Livingston, William."

[19] *Dictionary of American Biography*, s.v. "Iredell, James."

[20] Philo A. Goodwin, *Biography of Andrew Jackson* (New York: R. Hart Towner, 1833), p. 4.

he was created for. Each child was designed to excel in certain areas. As we observed our kids and prayed over them, we tried to understand what that direction was. We wanted to help them pursue those areas and begin to developing those skills and to prepare for a career and for adulthood.

We observed that Keith's desire for a "pooder" when he was three grew into a genuine interest in computers as he grew older. We saw this as an opportunity to help him develop this interest and his skills. The internet was relatively new when Keith reached his early teen years. I still had no idea what the internet was, and I entered the computer world with my feet dragging, but John was keeping up on the new technology, and decided to challenge Keith. John gave him a budget and let him use our computer to study and to order parts and build his own computer. Keith took the bait and ran with it. He was motivated to study and learn, and soon built his very own computer. It worked fairly well, and John only had to make a few tweaks in it to get it running great.

We also noticed Keith was interested in designing things on the computer, so his birthday and Christmas gifts became tools to help learn how to do design work. His really good friend Stephen also had similar interests, so they spent much of their time learning how to use new design programs and tools. They also became interested in photography. They were both highly motivated and spent several years developing these very useful skills. By the time Keith and Stephen were in college, they both had many years of design experience under their belt. Keith was already very experienced using the programs that were taught in his university classes, therefore he was able to spend much of his time helping other students learn these skills. Stephen went on to become an engineer, and Keith became a graphic designer and photographer.

As we observed Stacie, we discovered her love for people and for serving others. We encouraged her to be involved in mission trips, a leadership training internship, and service projects. She developed her people skills and leadership skills and is using them in her job today.

I know it is very unusual not have huge issues when it comes to young love, and I don't know why this was not a big problem for us. It just wasn't, and it probably had a lot to do with the nature of our kids or simply the grace of God. Again, I admit I do not have much experience with teenagers and dating, and I don't have solutions to those kinds of problems.

When each of our children knew the time was right, they pursued friendships with a different perspective. They began pursuing marriage when the time was appropriate. They still had some struggles, but we are pleased that they sought after and continued to follow the Lord.

*Kitty Spencer*

# Chapter 9

# Work Ethic

My husband and I wondered if we had made the right decision hiring yet another contractor for a house project. The hood over our oven needed to be replaced, and it was going to be a tricky project.

We were a little hesitant to hire someone because the previous two contractors did a poor job. For example, had we not been watching carefully, the highly recommended roofers would have cut right through the trusses while installing some solar tubes, compromising the integrity of the roof. (One brought some duct tape and a can of texture spray to fix his misplaced hole in the ceiling. I asked him what the duct tape was for. He said someone told him he would need tape and texture for the drywall. (Need I say more?) The floor installers we hired also did a terrible job by leaving gaps and uneven areas in the floor.

I had lost confidence in contractors, but this time it was different. A pleasant young man and his assistant arrived precisely on time. He explained everything he was going to do, and he worked quickly and efficiently. We were impressed and my hope was restored. I thought about the stark difference between the work ethic of this young man who did a terrific job and took pride in his work and the others who were in a hurry to finish and did poor work.

Does God really care about our work ethic? Is it something we need to focus on while training our children? Good attitudes toward work do not come automatically. In fact, they vary from person to person and from culture to culture. For instance: In Rome during Jesus' time, work was not valued. About two-thirds of the people were slaves and were expected to do all the work. Cicero, a first century Roman said working for one's livelihood was "unbecoming to a gentleman." In ancient Athens, manual labor was considered "loathsome" by the upper class. This repulsion toward work permeated many societies. In America, however, we generally tend to think of work as a virtue.

Scripture is not ambiguous concerning the value of work. God calls on each of us to work hard and to use our talents wisely, whether those abilities are small or great. God expects us to work if we are able. Paul told the Thessalonians: *"For even when we were with you, we would give you this command: If anyone is not willing to work, let him not eat."* (2 Thessalonians 3:10, ESV). Jesus demonstrated to his disciples a pattern of work and servanthood when he washed their feet and commended them to do likewise. Scripture is full of examples of hard work being commended. God created man and immediately gave him a purpose and a job to do.

> **God blessed them and said to them, "Be fruitful and increase in number; fill the earth and subdue it. Rule over the fish of the sea and the birds of the air and over every living creature that moves on the ground." (Genesis 1:28, NIV)**

> **The LORD God took the man and put him in the Garden of Eden to work it and take care of it. (Genesis 2:15, NIV)**

God continues to commend work. He admonishes us to do our work well, to work hard, to be skillful, to be persistent, and to work with integrity. He also warns against laziness, sloppy work, and dishonesty.

*Well-spoken words bring satisfaction; well-done work has its own reward. (Proverbs 12:14, The Message)*

*Better to be ordinary and work for a living than act important and starve in the process. (Proverbs 12:9, The Message)*

*Hard work always pays off; mere talk puts no bread on the table. (Proverbs 14:23, The Message)*

*Slack habits and sloppy work are as bad as vandalism. (Proverbs 18:9, The Message)*

*Observe people who are good at their work— skilled workers are always in demand and admired; they don't take a backseat to anyone. (Proverbs 22:29, The Message)*

*Committed and persistent work pays off; get-rich-quick schemes are rip-offs. (Proverbs 28:20, The Message)*

*GOD hates cheating in the marketplace; rigged scales are an outrage. (Proverbs 20:23, The Message)*

How do we instill a good work ethic in our children? We do want our kids to work hard and have integrity, but we do not want them to become workaholics or to be constantly stressed out because they expect too much from themselves.

I have discovered seven Biblical principles for teaching children a healthy work ethic and three additional principles to protect them from overworking. The following principles establish guidelines for work:

- Principle 1: Work heartily as unto the Lord.
- Principle 2: Be guided by integrity.
- Principle 3: Do what you say you are going to do.
- Principle 4: Be on time.

- Principle 5: Work with enthusiasm, regardless of how you feel at the moment.

- Principle 6: Turn and Look.

- Principle 7: Develop a servant's heart.

The next three principles help them to remain balanced and not become workaholics.

- Principle 8: Honor the Sabbath.

- Principle 9: Do not eat the bread of anxious toil.

- Principle 10: Make time for friends, family.

How do we help our children develop a good work ethic? Jesus spent three years walking with his disciples. He set an example for them. The absolute most important way to help children develop a proper work ethic is for parents to model a good one. They will learn far more from watching you than from anything you say. Next, Jesus deliberately taught them. He showed them what to do and then sent them out to do it. When they came back from doing a task, He commended them for what they did well, and when necessary, He encouraged them in ways they could improve. We can do the same with our children as we teach them Biblical principles concerning work.

## Principle 1 --Work heartily as unto the Lord

The *Parable of the Talents* in Matthew 25:14-30, tells the story of a man going on a journey who entrusted his property to his servants. He gave five talents (a certain amount of money) to one servant, two talents to another and one talent to another, each according to his ability. The man with five talents went and traded them and made five more talents. The man who had two talents made two more talents. But the man with only one talent dug a hole and hid his master's money in the ground. When the master returned, he said to the first two servants, "Well done, good and faithful servants. You have been faithful over little; I will set you over much. Enter into the joy of your master." The master said to the third servant, the one who buried the talent instead of using it "You wicked and slothful servant." The master then took the one talent from this slothful servant and gave it to the servant who had ten talents.

The master in the parable gave each servant a number of talents according to his own choosing. God, too, gives us talents and unique abilities according to His own choosing. He gives us everything we need in order to fulfill His call on our lives. It is important that we faithfully use these abilities the best we can, and it is equally important that we don't compare our abilities to others. God is our master and He has a purpose and a plan for each of us.

***For we are God's handiwork, created in Christ Jesus to do good works, which God prepared in advance for us to do. (Ephesians 2:10, NIV)***

Whether we are working in a prestigious position or perhaps caring for our own home, our work is worship to our God. He wants us to delight in our work and do our best. He says: "You shall rejoice before the Lord your God in all to which you put your hands," (Deuteronomy 18:12 NKJV). If we know we are working for God, we will do our best, regardless of who is watching us. We will also do our best even when no one else is watching.

Sometimes our work can seem tedious and unrewarding. This seems especially true when there are babies and young children in the home. You can change countless diapers, do piles of laundry and dishes and then turn around and they have to be done it again…. and again…and again. Doing these chores can be boring and feel thankless. For some reason, unknown to me, our Father in Heaven cherishes the moments we joyfully labor for Him in these menial tasks. We work for Him! Our God sees us. One of His names is "El Ro'I," which means "the God of Seeing."

*From the place of His dwelling He looks on all the inhabitants of the earth; He fashions their hearts individually; He considers all their works. (Psalm 33:14–15, NKJV)*

Can you imagine? He sees us and works diligently in our lives to fashion our hearts into His likeness. None of our frustrations, tears, sorrows or even boredom is wasted. Our God graciously takes these everyday circumstances, and like the potter with the clay, molds our hearts skillfully into His masterpiece. He asks us to treasure these moments doing tasks for Him. "Whatever you do, work heartily, as for the Lord and not for men," (Colossians 3:23, ESV). Make sure your kids understand this principle and that they know all their work is important to God.

### Principle 2 --Be Guided by Integrity

*The integrity of the upright shall guide them: But the perverseness of transgressors shall destroy them. (Proverbs 11:3, KJV)*

When someone is guided by integrity, he or she will make choices that are righteous, regardless of the consequences. Every day our children have to make choices, and many of those choices have moral components to them. If they choose to do what is right rather than what they feel like doing, or what is easier to do, or what is most convenient, they are walking in integrity. They will be people of noble character. If they can live by the motto, do the right thing next, they will be trustworthy and dependable.

What does it look like for someone to be guided by integrity? According to Collins English Dictionary, integrity is defined as: an adherence to moral principles; honesty. For the Christian, these principles are set forth in Scripture. These principles can be seen all around us. For example, suppose a five-year-old is at his friend's house and sees a piece of his favorite candy lying on table. He may be tempted to slip it into his pocket when no one is looking. He chooses not to because he knows it is wrong to steal. He is guided by integrity. Perhaps a teen has an important test he needs to pass in order to pass the class. He has an opportunity to cheat, thereby ensuring success, but he chooses not to cheat because he knows it is wrong. He is guided by integrity. Perhaps a boss threatens to fire a young employee if she won't lie for him, and she chooses not to lie. She is guided by integrity. Suppose someone is extremely angry about someone else and feels like gossiping, but chooses not to. He is guided by integrity. Suppose someone is tired and is tempted to take a shortcut on a job he is doing. He knows no one will ever know, but he chooses to do the job the correct way. He is guided by integrity.

Children do not learn to walk in integrity by accident. They need to see integrity modeled and they need to be trained. God's Word is like a plumb line. It is the standard by which moral standards and honesty are measured. As parents, we not only tried to model a life of integrity, we tried many ways to capture our children's hearts so they would desire to spend time in God's Word and want to guide their lives with it. One of our favorite approaches that generated enthusiasm in our devotional times was a monthly magazine subscription called *YouthWalk* by *Walk Thru the Bible Ministries*. It is a daily devotional which deals with topics such as temptation, depression, peer pressure, drugs, loneliness, friendship, faithfulness, and many others. It begins each lesson with a modern, easily relatable story about a relevant topic, followed by thought provoking questions, then solutions from Scripture. Our children would try to solve the problem presented in the story and then get to see if their solutions lined up with God's solutions as given in the Scriptures. They got increasingly better at finding godly solutions to problems. By diligently seeking God's guidance, every family can find a unique way to inspire their children to desire to know God through His Word, and in so doing, help these children to know how to walk in integrity.

I have a plan to get my new grandbaby excited about God and His Word. I am going to call it *Scripture Sleuthing.* After all, who doesn't love a good mystery? Grandma and Grandpa's house is going to be so much fun. We are going to read a story from the Bible together, then see how many clues there are that tell us about God. For instance, this morning I read Psalm 38. In verse 15 it said, "For I hope in You, O Lord; You will answer, O Lord my God." This tells us a lot about God. She will get to figure out all kinds of things from this passage. Where it says, "I hope in God," she will be able to understand that God gives us hope. "You will answer," tells her that God hears her and answers her. As a child, I always wondered whether or not God could really hear me. She will know He hears her. It also tells her she is important enough to God for Him to answer her. "O Lord, my God" tells her "my God" is a personal God. He is not just a God; He is her God.

When we read the story of David and Goliath, she will know that her God is powerful enough to slay giants. The story of Jonah will teach her God has a call on her life and He loves her and pursues her. Daniel in the Lion's Den will show her that He is stronger than the mighty beasts. The story of Samson will teach her that there are consequences to disobedience. Samson violated God's laws on many occasions and was controlled by sensuality, but God loved Samson and had much mercy on him. Even though there were consequences to Samson's sinful choices, such as having his eyes gouged out by the Philistines, God stayed with Samson. Through God's supernatural strength, Samson delivered Israel from the hands of the

Philistines. God listed Samson in the *Hall of Faith* in Hebrews 11 as one of those "who through faith subdued kingdoms, worked righteousness, obtained promises." My granddaughter is still a baby, but I have great plans for us. Right now I just sing to her, play with her, read to her, and laugh with her a lot. I love her giggles.

When I think about walking in integrity, I think about Adam and Eve. They walked in the garden in the cool of the day with God Himself. They basked in His presence. They experienced His peace. God personally taught them how to live. God loved them and He gave them purpose. Through God's Word and His Holy Spirit, like Adam and Eve, our children can walk with God.

> *Whoever has my commands and keeps them is the one who loves me. The one who loves me will be loved by my Father, and I too will love him and <u>show myself</u> to him. (John 14:21, NIV)*

This verse says God shows Himself to those who love Him. He will guide them, love them, and show Himself to them. "I will instruct you and teach you in the way you should go; I will guide you with My eye." (Psalm 32:8, NKJV) He will personally teach them to walk in integrity.

## Principle 3 --Do What You Say You Are Going to Do.

> *God is not a human being, and he will not lie. He is not a human, and he does not change his mind. What he says he will do, he does. What he promises, he makes come true. (Numbers 23:19, NCV)*

Words should mean something. People who do what they say they are going to do are dependable. They stand out and get noticed. They gain a reputation for being trustworthy. The opposite is also true. Too often, people don't follow through with what they say. Unfortunately, this is much too common, even in the church. For instance, my husband and I were teaching a finance class at our church which included a short video for each lesson. We were unfamiliar the new audio-visual system so we asked a couple of the church interns who had signed up for the class if they would play the video for us each week. They agreed to help us, but failed to show up over half of the time and did not let us know ahead of time they were not coming. We muddled through and eventually got the system to work, but it wasted a lot of our time and the rest of the class's time. Sadly, we learned not to rely on those interns. (We probably should have talked to them about doing what they say they are going to do.) We also noticed that people who sign up to teach Sunday school classes or usher or to do other various jobs around the church often fail show up. This leaves those who are at church scurrying to find replacements. This should not happen! Model dependability and expect it from your children.

Begin at a very early age to teach children to follow through when they say they will do something. Do not let them back out of anything unless it is an absolute emergency that they don't have control over. God does what He says He will do, and we need to, also.

## Principle 4 -- Be on Time

*There is an occasion for everything, and a time for every activity under heaven: (Ecclesiastes 3:1, HCSB)*

Being on time is a common courtesy. It demonstrates respect for other people. If we have arranged to meet someone at a particular time and we are late, their time is wasted as they wait for us, and this indicates we don't think their time is important. If we are late for a meeting, a class or some other group, we interrupt the speaker and the attendees. If we are late for a job, people often lose confidence in us, and in many companies, it is grounds for being fired. Being on time is a polite and proper way to treat others, but it is not always easy.

For some reason it always takes me longer to get ready to go somewhere than I think it will. If I plan to leave the house by 8:15, I can't seem to be out the door until 8:30. This used to drive my husband crazy. He does not like to be late, and he gets frustrated when he has to wait for me. We finally came up with a solution. If we have to leave at 8:15, I set a goal of being ready by 8:00. I have this vision of myself all ready to leave, shoes on, jacket on, purse in hand, fifteen minutes early, sitting with a good book, relaxing while John finishes getting ready. It hasn't happened yet! I scramble out the door at the last minute, but at least I am seldom late anymore.

The best way to help our children to be on time is to make it a family habit. Make it "normal" to arrive five to ten minutes early to every event. This provides a margin for the unexpected, and it relieves stress and anxiety from our everyday lives. It is not hard. It just needs to become a habit.

## Principle 5 --Work with Enthusiasm

*At last the wall was completed to half its height around the entire city, for the people had worked with enthusiasm. (Nehemiah 4:6, NLT)*

Eeyore, a character in the *Winnie-the-Pooh* books by A. A. Milne, is a pessimistic, gloomy, depressed, old, grey stuffed donkey. He is really cute and he can get away with being mopey, but he is not real. When real people act like Eeyore, they can have an effect on others similar to that of a doctor giving a cancer diagnosis. They can quickly change the atmosphere in an entire gathering. They carry with them heaviness and gloom, and it quickly rubs off onto others. On the other hand, someone with the joy of the Lord is like sunshine coming into a room on a cloudy day.

God tells us to rejoice before the Lord our God in all that we do. My friend Janice does just that. Although her past has been painful and difficult, and she suffers from many health issues, she is full of joy. She is on disability because of frequent seizures, painful arthritis, and other serious health issues, but she has determined to believe God has a good plan for her. God says in Psalm 23: "Surely goodness and mercy shall follow me all the days of my life; And I will dwell in the house of the LORD forever." (Psalm 23:6, NKJV) She believes Him and is joyful because of it. Because of the health issues, she has been unable to maintain a full-time job. However, through some amazing circumstances she was able to get an on-call position as a dishwasher at a retirement center. With this job, if she is well enough to work when she is called, she says "Yes." If not, she says "No." She believes this opportunity is a gift from God.

Janice immediately brought her enthusiasm into the workplace. Because of her attitude, what started out as a dishwashing position soon expanded into food preparation as well as serving meals to the residents. She quickly learned each of their names and addressed them personally. She brought joy and smiles into the entire dining room.

I know Janice doesn't always feel well and deals with many difficulties, but you can't tell by watching her. She serves the Lord by serving others with love and enthusiasm, regardless of how she feels at the moment. We can encourage our children to do likewise by modeling enthusiasm and by teaching them that life is not all about them. We don't need any more Eeyores around. Life is about serving Jesus by loving and serving others. Enthusiasm really matters.

## Principle 6 --Turn and Look

I am convinced that the words "turn and look" will be forever ingrained in the deep recesses of my children's brains. I am sure that even after I am long gone, they will "hear" these words from their mother inside their heads every time they finish a project or leave a room. Parents should not have to pick up after their children! Kids can learn to turn around and look at where they have been working or playing or eating etc. and make sure the area is cleaned.

"Turning and looking" is similar to being in an airplane when it is time to land and the flight attendant says to "clear the tray." It is easy. Everyone in the plane puts away their things and puts their tray in the upright position. When our kids are finished doing something, they need to remember to turn and look, and make sure they have cleared their work area. After taking a shower, their towel should be hung up and their clothes put away. When they finish making a sandwich, the bread, peanut butter and jelly should be put away and the counter wiped. When they are finished doing a project on the kitchen table, the supplies should be put away.

Just a little side note here: Some projects may take days or weeks to finish, but it is still possible to tidy up the work area when finishing up for the day. This doesn't mean, however, that it is okay to begin a lot of projects and then just leave them unfinished. A sign of maturity is actually finishing a project before starting a new one. If you have creative kids, ideas flow like maple syrup on a hot day. It is easy to begin something new, but it takes discipline to complete tasks. Painting a bedroom or building a bookshelf may sound like a great idea and can be fun to start, but finishing can begin to feel like drudgery. Why finish painting when you could be building your own pellet gun shooting range in the backyard? That would be so much more fun right now. Why hammer in those last few shelves in the bookshelf when you could be building a track for a remote-control car? Finishing the bookshelf may not be as much fun as starting the new shooting range project. It takes self-discipline and it is the right thing to do.

My daughter has begun early teaching her young one to clean up after herself. When she is done playing, my daughter sings her a wonderful little "clean up" song from the children's show *Barney*. The baby doesn't quite get the hang of it yet. Last time we sang it, I proceeded to put her little toys in a box, and she quickly removed them all. We will keep playing that game. Eventually she will learn. This is child training. It all takes time and consistency.

When they get older and you see things left out, you don't need to yell, stomp your feet, and make threats. Call them to the area and say, "Turn and look." (This is their clue to see what they left out and put it away.) They will get so sick of hearing those words that they will finally figure out all by themselves that you will not pick up after them and that it is much easier for them to just turn, look, and put things away than it is to constantly be reminded. And the best part of this entire plan is that when they are away from home, they will still hear that annoying little voice when they finish a project or leave a room saying, "Turn and look."

## Principle 7 --Develop a Servant's Heart

> *For you have been called to live in freedom, my brothers and sisters. But don't use your freedom to satisfy your sinful nature. Instead, use your freedom to serve one another in love. (Galatians 5:13, NLT)*

When my son was in second grade, his classroom did a musical about Nehemiah. A line from one the songs in the play would go through my mind whenever we would see and opportunity to help someone, and I would sing it with the kids. The words are: "If you want to be great in God's kingdom, learn to be a servant of all." This kind of attitude brings joy to our hearts and smiles on people's faces. If we saw someone with their hands full trying to open a door, we'd open it. If we saw a little old lady drop a piece of paper, (ooh, that could be me now) we would pick it up for her. This became normal for them. It is easy to fall into the trap of being more concerned about "What is in it for me?", but we should: **"*Do nothing out of selfish ambition or vain conceit. Rather, in humility value others above yourselves,*"** (Philippians 2:3, NIV) There is never a shortage of opportunities to "serve one another in love."

## Principle 8 --Honor the Sabbath

God is a God of order. He sets boundaries around our lives to protect us from harming ourselves. He wants us to eat, but not overeat. He wants us to sleep, but not oversleep. He wants us to work, but not overwork. God gave the children of Israel the Ten Commandments in order to teach them to live well. They had just spent four hundred years in slavery in Egypt. They had been afflicted with hard labor by cruel taskmasters day after day. Imagine the relief and joy they experienced when God provided for a Sabbath day of rest every week. What a gift they received! That gift is still available to us today. If we cannot finish our work in six days, we are doing more than God has called us to do. Perhaps it is time to eliminate some of our self-appointed responsibilities. God knows how our bodies function, and He knows we need a day of rest each week. He is a good God, and He has given us the marvelous gift of a guilt free day of rest. Wow! What a blessing.

## Principle 9 --Do Not Eat the Bread of Anxious Toil

*It is in vain that you rise up early and go late to rest, eating the bread of anxious toil; for he gives to his beloved sleep. (Psalm 127:2, ESV)*

I learned a lot about trusting God to take care of our needs from my friend Carolyn. She is amazing. She is a single mom of two children. In order to make a living while staying home with her children, she took in foster children. This is really not a very abundant source of income, and barely covered the costs of each child she fostered. That didn't matter. She had another source. She knew her Father in Heaven loved her and her children far more than you can imagine. He is a good Father. He owns the cattle on every hill, (see Psalm 59:10). She knew her God would supply all their needs according to all His riches in glory, (see Philippians 4:19). She did the best she could with what she had and trusted God for whatever else she needed. Rather than being anxious and fussing over shortages, she simply praised God and asked for what she needed.

*Be anxious for nothing, but in everything by prayer and supplication, with thanksgiving, let your requests be made known to God. (Philippians 4:6, NKJV)*

I have a tendency to worry when I foresee some shortage, such as unexpected bills, getting laid off from work, a coming national financial crisis, etc. But time after time, I watched as God abundantly supplied for Carolyn's family in miraculous ways. One time she was really excited about having gotten a turkey for Thanksgiving. She was talking to a friend who didn't have one. This touched her heart and she asked her kids if it would be okay to give away their turkey. They all agreed it was a good thing to do, so they gave it to the friend. That evening, two frozen turkeys appeared on her front porch. God is generous.

Be careful not to lie awake with worry. Jesus wants us to balance our hard work with peace and rest.

*This is why I tell you to never be worried about your life, for all that you need will be provided, such as food, water, clothing—everything your body needs. Isn't there more to your life than a meal? Isn't your body more than clothing? Look at all the birds—do you think they worry about their existence? They don't plant or reap or store up food, yet your heavenly Father provides them each with food. Aren't you much more valuable to your Father than they? So, which one of you by worrying could add anything to your life? And why would you worry about your clothing? Look at all the beautiful flowers of the field. They don't work or toil, and yet not even Solomon in all his splendor was robed in beauty more than one of these! So if God has clothed the meadow with hay, which is here for such a short time and then dried up and burned, won't he provide for you the clothes you need— even though you live with such little faith? So then, forsake your worries! Why would you say, "What will we eat?" or "What will we drink?" or "What will we wear?" For that is what the unbelievers chase after. Doesn't your heavenly Father already know the things your bodies require? So above all, constantly chase after the realm of God's kingdom and the righteousness that proceeds from him. Then all these less important things will be given to you abundantly. Refuse to worry about tomorrow, but deal with each challenge that comes your way, one day at a time. Tomorrow will take care of itself. (Matthew 6:25-34, TPT)*

Instead of worrying, begin praising God for His faithfulness. Do you have food each day? Do you have a roof over your head? Do you have clothing? Do you have people in your life who care about you? Thank God daily for the wonderful blessings you do have. Teach your kids to do the same.

## Principal 10 --Make Time for Friends and Family

My parents had the following saying in my family while I was growing up: "When you turn eighteen, we will break your plate." I am quite certain they intended this to mean they wanted us to grow up and be responsible and independent. Unfortunately, that's not what I heard. I heard: "When you turn eighteen, you are on your own. Do not ask for help, advice, or anything else. We are breaking ties." This idea was re-enforced shortly after John and I were married, and I had a medical emergency. John called my dad to ask what he should do. My dad responded by saying. "I don't know. You figure it out. She is your problem now." I think he wanted to show us we could handle it, but we both foolishly picked up an offense and decided, "Okay, we are on our own for now on." I know this is not what God intends for families. Families should be a wonderful support system.

The ancient Israelites, God's chosen people, knew how to make time for family and friends. God had designed the family, and He had commanded many feasts to be celebrated regularly. The feasts and festivals of Israel included the Feast of Pentecost, the feast of Trumpets, the Day of Atonement, Feast of Tabernacles, Hanukkah, Purim, and many more celebrations. These feasts commemorated events, celebrated God's faithfulness, and placed great emphasis on community involvement. God had initiated these activities. They were part of the fabric of Israel. He knew what was important and good for His people. These feasts added a spiritual dimension to the Israelites' lives and provided a means of unity for the nation throughout generations under the guidance and protection of the Lord.

It is just as important for us to spend time with family and friends now as it was in ancient Israel. There is a fascinating story in Malcolm Gladwell's *New York Time's* bestseller, *Outliers.* It tells of a physician who visited the small town of Roseto, Pennsylvania, and discovered that in this community, very few of the residents had heart disease. Also, there was virtually no suicide, no alcoholism, no drug addiction, and very little crime. They didn't even have peptic ulcers. Generally, people were dying of old age, nothing more.

A study was initiated by this physician who enlisted help from colleagues, medical students and sociology graduate students from the University of Oklahoma. They wanted to discover if the well-being of this community was a result of their genetics, their location, their environment, their dietary practices, exercise, or their spiritual life. After extensive research they found some surprising results. They discovered that the people of Roseto did come from healthy European ancestry, but the Rosetan's close relatives living in other parts of America did not experience the same health and longevity.

Next, they looked at environment. The people in other communities that lived near Roseto, in similar environments, did not exhibit the remarkable statistics of Roseto residents. They next considered dietary practices and found the practices of these Rosetan people were typical of many Americans. They ate processed foods, abundant sweets, high fat diets, and many smoked regularly and struggled with obesity. Also, they didn't exercise much. It wasn't their diet and exercise. Their spiritual life was typical of many other Catholic communities around the nation. They attended mass at Our Lady of Mount Carmel regularly, but didn't seem to do anything out of the ordinary. It wasn't their religion that made them healthy.

The researchers eventually began to realize that community made the difference. They were a tight, close knit group of people. They visited each other often as they walked through the streets. They had backyard barbeques together. Often times, three generations of a family would live under one roof. There was great respect for grandparents. Evenings were spent sitting on porches or in living rooms together visiting one another. They had a powerful, protective social structure. The Bible addresses healthy community in Romans 12:10.

*Be kindly affectioned one to another with brotherly love; in honour preferring one another. (Romans 12:10, KJV)*

God does not intend for us to live isolated lives. He made us social beings. As this study shows, being in community affects our health and well-being. We need one another.

We tried to make this concept a part of our family life. We made it very clear to our children we would always be there for them, and that family is important. We want our kids to see themselves as part of a generational heritage, and we want them to understand that their decisions can affect generations to come. We also meet regularly with friends just to have fun and relax. Work is important, but making time to enjoy friends and family brings a healthy balance to life.

Recently, my husband and I were at Lowe's home improvement store, when we noticed a dynamic young employee helping an older, rather frail customer. The customer needed several bags of concrete, some lumber and assorted other items. The employee had short, spikey, purple hair and a smile that seemed larger than life. She assured the customer she would help her find everything on the list. The customer wondered out loud how she would get all of the supplies into her truck. The employee told her, "Don't you worry about a thing. I will take care of you and make sure everything gets into your truck." I was so impressed. This little gal appeared to have a great work ethic. I wondered if her parents had purposely trained her to do her job with enthusiasm. Had she been trained to work heartily as unto the Lord? Was she guided by integrity? Does she do what she says she is going to do? Is she on time regularly? Does she finish her jobs and clean up after herself? Does she honor the Sabbath? Does she rest in the Lord rather than worrying? Does she make time for family and friends? I have a hunch, maybe they did train her in these things. This kind of training will set our children apart and give them a huge advantage as they set out on their own.

# Chapter 10

# Prayer

It seemed like a normal evening. I had just started to get ready for bed when suddenly I had excruciating pain in my abdomen. I walked the few steps to my bed and lay down. I called for my husband and asked him to call 911. I told him this may be the end. We knew that living with Vascular Ehlers Danlos carried the risk of ruptured blood vessels, and something major had just happened. John called, and the ambulance was there in minutes. We were immediately taken to the hospital. I am so grateful for pain medication. They gave me Dilaudid, and the pain let up. I thought about meeting Jesus face to face and actually got a little excited. Then I thought about John and the kids living without me and decided I didn't like that idea. I told the Lord I would really like to live longer. It would break my heart to think about how they would feel if I died. Then I told Him, "Lord, You are good, You love us, and You are in control. It is all up to You."

John called some friends and asked them to pray. They passed the news on to others who prayed. After arriving at the hospital, the staff did a lot of poking and prodding, and an abdominal ultrasound followed by a CT scan. A physician came in with a worried look on his face, but I felt at peace. He said I had a dissected aorta that was bleeding into my abdomen. My blood count, which was normally around 42, had quickly dropped to 31. They were going to send me to the trauma center at Harborview in Seattle, one of the best trauma centers in the country. Because it was now in the wee hours of the morning and traffic was minimal, they decided an ambulance would be faster than a helicopter. On the ninety mile an hour trip down the freeway, the nurse in the ambulance told me how God had miraculously saved her own life after a serious heart issue, then she prayed for me. I felt like God Himself was encouraging me, and I continued to experience God's peace.

We arrived at the trauma center, and I waited for several hours. Finally, one of the doctors told me that several top vascular surgeons in the nation had been discussing my case, and he said he was sorry, but they could not treat my condition because of the location of the tear and because of the Ehler's Danlos. They would arrange for me to sign up for hospice and do the best they could to keep me comfortable until I died, which could take minutes, hours or possibly days. That wasn't really what I wanted to hear. They kept me in the hospital a few more days, monitoring the pain and trying to keep me comfortable. A hospice nurse and social worker visited me and told me what to expect. They then sent me home with a bag full of end-of-life medications and a hospice handbook.

When we arrived home, I asked the Lord if I was going to die soon. Immediately after praying, I walked into our back bedroom which we had transformed into an office. On the floor, in the middle of the room, my grandmother's old *Book of Psalms* was lying opened. I thought that was strange. That little pocket-sized Bible had been on the shelf, untouched for over five years. How did it get on the floor? I picked it up and looked at it. It was opened to Psalm 41. When I read it, I knew God had answered my question and somehow made that Bible fall opened on the floor. Could an angel have put it there? Maybe. John and I tried several times to drop it and see if it would open to that Psalm. It did not. It just kept falling apart. Psalm 41 read:

*Verse 1: "Happy is he who is considerate of the needy and poor." (We had been doing work with the poor)*

*Verse 2: "The Lord will rescue him in the day of trouble." (This was definitely a day of trouble)*

*Verse 3: "The Lord will preserve him and keep him alive," (This was the best news I'd heard in quite a while) "and make him happy upon earth," (In spite of all that had happened, I still felt happy. This happiness surprised me, and I was thankful for the unexplainable joy.) "and will not deliver him to the will of his enemies." (Jesus said in John 10:10 that the enemy, the devil, came to kill, steal and destroy, but Jesus came so we may have abundant life.)*

*Verse 4: "The Lord will support him on his bed of pain: and in his sickness remove all his weakness." (I am definitely experiencing the support of the Lord on my bed of sickness, and I am continuing to trust Him to remove all of my weaknesses.)*

I believe God personally told me He was going to keep me alive and heal my weaknesses. I later found out that prayer had literally gone out all over the world for me. My son-in-law's parents had sent word to Lutheran prayer groups in many other countries. Many others told me they had put in a prayer request to other international ministries. My husband goes to "Manprayer" at our church where between sixty and eighty men gather each week and cry out to the Lord. They prayed for me. My friends and family prayed and asked for prayer from their respective churches. I could not be more thankful and more blessed. I know God answered these prayers.

Within just a few weeks, I graduated from hospice and began walking outside for exercise. On one of my walks, one of the pastors from a local congregation was driving by and saw me. He did a U-turn and pulled his car over to talk to me. He said his church had been praying for me and was delighted to see how God answered. I thanked him and told him what a blessing it was to be cared about by him and his church. God is amazing.

At the time of this writing, it has been two years since this incident took place, and I am doing well. The last CT scan showed that I am healing well. I am believing that God will continue to heal "all of my weaknesses."

One of the most important things we can do while raising our children is to pray for them. Perhaps you have wondered if prayer really makes a difference? When you pray, does God hear you? Does He really do anything to change what is happening on earth in response to your prayers? Does He care about the little things? Sometimes we pray for someone and we see an answer. Was it God, or was it a coincidence? Sometimes we pray and nothing seems to happen. Did God ignore those prayers? How do we know for sure if God hears and answers our prayers?

We know because God speaks to us through His Word.

> *O LORD, You have searched me and known me. You know my sitting down and my rising up; You understand my thought afar off. You comprehend my path and my lying down, and are acquainted with all my ways. For there is not a word on my tongue, but behold, O LORD, You know it altogether. (Psalm 139:1–4, NKJV)*

God is acquainted with everything about us and He hears us. He says:

> *Confess your trespasses to one another, and pray for one another, that you may be healed. The effective, fervent prayer of a righteous man avails much. Elijah was a man with a nature like ours, and he prayed earnestly that it would not rain; and it did not rain on the land for three years and six months. And he prayed again, and the*

***heaven gave rain, and the earth produced its fruit. (James
5:16–18, NKJV)***

The fervent prayer of a righteous man avails much. If we are
believers and have confessed our sin and turned from it, God forgives
us and we qualify as righteous, just like Elijah was.

***For God made the only one who did not know sin to
become sin for us, so that we who did not know
righteousness might become the righteousness of God
through our union with Him. (2 Corinthians 5:21, TPT)***

The righteousness of Christ is imparted to us because of our union
with Him, and God says that the prayer of the righteous avails much.
Yes, our prayers avail much! Continue to pray for your children and
partner with God in all you do. He is powerful and faithful.

This book gives some ideas, examples, and principles for raising
children, but even more importantly, I hope it encourages you to seek
the Lord with all your heart, mind, soul, and strength as you raise
them. He will give you everything you need to guide them well. And
finally, rest and rejoice in the goodness and faithfulness of our
Heavenly Father. He is the perfect parent! Enjoy the children He
gave you to raise.

Kitty Spencer is available for book interviews and personal appearances. For more information contact:

Kitty Spencer
C/O Advantage Books
P.O. Box 160847
Altamonte Springs, FL 32716
info@advbooks.com

To purchase additional copies of these books, visit our bookstore at:
www.advbookstore.com

**A**dvantage
BOOKS

Longwood, Florida, USA
"we bring dreams to life" ™
www.advbookstore.com

www.ingramcontent.com/pod-product-compliance
Lightning Source LLC
LaVergne TN
LVHW051127080426
835510LV00018B/2266